"From the first page to the last, this book sparkles with good humor and engaging wisdom. In smart, funny ways, Wilkens shows how humor is the ideal approach to our 'magnificently paradoxical' human condition as spiritual animals, somewhere between angels and apes. 'If you don't believe God has a sense of humor,' he writes, 'just look in the mirror.' He includes not only Augustine, Aquinas, Luther, Calvin, and modern theologians but also humorists like Jim Gaffigan, Gary Larsen of *The Far Side*, and the writers of *The Big Bang Theory*. Arguing that our unique ability among animals to appreciate humor is linked to our rationality, moral sensibility, and aesthetic sense, Wilkens makes a good case for adding a fourth transcendental to the true, the good, and the beautiful—the funny. Along the way, he provides comedic interpretations of biblical books like Jonah and Esther and others in the New Testament. This is the best Christian understanding of humor to date—and by far the funniest."

John Morreall, author of *Comedy, Tragedy, and Religion*

"Steve Wilkens is funny in many ways—but God? In this funny but also serious guide, Wilkens shows what humor is and how the Bible, theology, church folks, and yes, even God, are indeed funny. Who knew? This book is even funnier than the six-volume *Anchor Yale Bible Dictionary*, at a fraction of the cost! You should buy it."

Alan G. Padgett, professor of systematic theology at Luther Seminary

"We Christians live between the deadly serious crucifixion and the incredibly exhilarating resurrection. One leads us to somber reflections on our mortality, injustice, and the gifts of grace and forgiveness. The other leads us to ponder immortality, to live with courage, and yes, to consider the utter hilarity of God entering death to bring life, of becoming human so we could become godly, and of telling stories (like Job, Jonah, and the parables of Jesus) so we could find the mysteries of life. Over the years of teaching the New Testament, I am convinced that humor, sometimes subtle and indirect and other times overt and direct, is found in the New Testament and can be used to enlighten our faith. It takes no imagination to consider those overhearing Jesus give it to the political and religious leaders poking one another in the ribs, and one can't read Paul's letter to Philemon and not feel the clever moves Paul makes to convince the man to welcome his runaway slave home. There it is: utterly serious dimensions of life-opening grace through the gift of humor. The funniest evening I ever had with theologians was in Baltimore, and Steve Wilkens was in the middle of it. Every pastor and professor needs to read this book, perhaps a few pages at a time before speaking to humans who can know God's ways through humor. Hilarity is the reverse side of serious."

Scot McKnight, Julius R. Mantey Chair of New Testament, Northern Seminary

T0346502

"Mark Twain said, 'Show me someone who knows what's funny and I'll show you someone who knows what isn't.' Steve Wilkens knows what's funny, and he knows what is profound. I was so taken by this marvelous book that I read it twice; once for the jokes—*conveniently italicized*—and once for his refreshing look at key theological themes. From peekaboo to punch lines, humor is a form of surprise. Can anything be more surprising than a God who exists as three, steps into human flesh, defeats death by dying—before the ultimate peekaboo of Easter morning? *What's So Funny About God?* is the best book I've read this year. I just wish I read more so that that would be even higher praise."

Gary W. Moon, director of the Martin Family Institute and Dallas Willard Center for Christian Spiritual Formation at Westmont College, author of *Becoming Dallas Willard*

"Steve Wilkens's *What's So Funny About God?* adds fresh insight to the study of religion and humor. It is playful, thought provoking, and generous with funny quotes and stories. Wilkens takes devices of humor such as incongruity, surprise, paradox, and reversal and uses them to explore theological themes and the church year, especially Christmas and Holy Week. He also opens out the funny features of the biblical stories of Abraham and Sarah, Jonah, Esther, and varied New Testament texts. The book demonstrates and invites us to new ways of thinking."

Howard R. Macy, professor emeritus of religion and biblical studies, George Fox University

STEVE WILKENS

WHAT'S SO FUNNY ABOUT GOD

?

A THEOLOGICAL LOOK AT HUMOR

ivp Academic

An imprint of InterVarsity Press
Downers Grove, Illinois

InterVarsity Press
P.O. Box 1400, Downers Grove, IL 60515-1426
ivpress.com
email@ivpress.com

InterVarsity Press® is the book-publishing division of InterVarsity Christian Fellowship/USA®, a movement of students and faculty active on campus at hundreds of universities, colleges, and schools of nursing in the United States of America, and a member movement of the International Fellowship of Evangelical Students. For information about local and regional activities, visit intervarsity.org.

Scripture quotations, unless otherwise noted, are from the New Revised Standard Version of the Bible, copyright 1989 by the Division of Christian Education of the National Council of the Churches of Christ in the USA. Used by permission. All rights reserved.

Cover design and artwork: David Fassett
Interior design: Jeanna Wiggins

ISBN 978-0-8308-5267-3 (print)
ISBN 978-0-8308-5545-2 (digital)

Printed in the United States of America ∞

InterVarsity Press is committed to ecological stewardship and to the conservation of natural resources in all our operations. This book was printed using sustainably sourced paper.

Library of Congress Cataloging-in-Publication Data

Names: Wilkens, Steve, 1955- author.

Title: What's so funny about God? : a theological look at humor / Steve Wilkens.

Description: Downers Grove, Illinois : IVP Academic, an imprint of InterVarsity Press, [2019] | Includes bibliographical references and index.

Identifiers: LCCN 2019029423 (print) | LCCN 2019029424 (ebook) | ISBN 9780830852673 (paperback) | ISBN 9780830855452 (ebook)

Subjects: LCSH: Wit and humor—Religious aspects—Christianity. | Wit and humor in the Bible.

Classification: LCC BR115.H84 W53 2019 (print) | LCC BR115.H84 (ebook) | DDC 230.02/07—dc23

LC record available at https://lccn.loc.gov/2019029423

LC ebook record available at https://lccn.loc.gov/2019029424

| P | 22 | 21 | 20 | 19 | 18 | 17 | 16 | 15 | 14 | 13 | 12 | 11 | 10 | 9 | 8 | 7 | 6 | 5 | 4 | 3 | 2 | 1 |
| Y | 39 | 38 | 37 | 36 | 35 | 34 | 33 | 32 | 31 | 30 | 29 | 28 | 27 | 26 | 25 | 24 | 23 | 22 | 21 | 20 | 19 |

CONTENTS

TO MY BROTHER-IN-LAW

Randy Whitcomb, MD

Running the race with perseverance

ACKNOWLEDGMENTS

None of the book projects I've undertaken up to this point has relied so heavily on the support and patience of family, friends, and colleagues, and I am truly grateful for the advice, feedback, and encouragement of so many. Indeed, the scope of those who have offered help is so broad that I know names will be omitted that surely should be here. I'll trust in your forgiveness where that has occurred.

First and foremost, my thanks to my wife, Debra, and children, Zack and Zoe. Over the years, they have been subjected to frequent barrages of "dad humor" and have been gracious enough to translate them as exactly what they are: awkward attempts to express my deep love for them. I forgive all three for erroneously insisting that sometimes I have a tendency to tell the same joke more than once.

A heavy debt of gratitude is owed to my colleagues in the School of Theology at Azusa Pacific University. They have helped me field-test jokes and quips, read portions of drafts, and acted as a sounding board for ideas, sometimes involuntarily so. Key among those individuals are Don Thorsen, Gregg Modor, Roger White, Justin Smith, Paul Shrier, and Keith Reeves, who put up with a lot of discussion about humor and theology during coffee breaks and cafeteria meals. Brian Lugioyo, Rob Muthiah, Kelly Thomas, Deona Hairston, Jill MacLaren, Sarah Montez, Jacque Winston, Barbara Hayes, and many other staff and faculty colleagues found themselves trapped behind desks and unable to escape my requests for ideas and responses. Nonetheless, all kindly offered feedback on snippets of humor. It is such a privilege to work with people who are not just highly competent at their work but are truly nice folks.

Several of my colleagues have been quite helpful in sharing their deep knowledge of Scripture. Of particular note, Justin Smith, Fed Roth, Eunny Lee, Bob Mullins, Traci Birge, Keith Reeves, Tim Finlay, and Bill Yarchin have all provided guidance on the nuances of Scripture that elude amateur exegetes such as myself. Readers of this book will no doubt conclude that I should have consulted their advice on numerous other issues, and they will be right.

I have been blessed to teach philosophy at Azusa Pacific University for the past thirty-two years and appreciate the research and writing opportunities they provided through my sabbatical, a CREV Fellowship, and the summer writers' retreat.

Finally, my history with IVP Academic stretches back almost thirty years, and my appreciation for their expertise, patience, and kindness continues unabated. I want to express special thanks to my editors—David Congdon, who was willing to take on an outside-the-box book idea, and Jon Boyd, who ushered the project through the final stages. Their wise guidance and the skills of the entire team have once again smoothed the path through the long process.

INTRODUCTION

PROFESSIONAL COURTESY

> **Why don't sharks attack lawyers?**
> **Professional courtesy.**

Of course, we can also turn this joke around and get a different result:

> **Why do sharks attack lawyers?**
> **They don't like the competition.**

Theology usually doesn't grant much professional courtesy to humor. Don't get me wrong. Christians, surprisingly, are almost like normal people; most of us seem to like humor. It's sprinkled throughout our everyday conversation, and we watch TV sitcoms as much as other groups. If you're looking for church jokes, a quick internet search reveals that we have found plenty to laugh about in this niche of our lives. When it comes to finding thoughtful Christian reflection on the topic of humor, though (to modify the late Rodney Dangerfield's signature line): "Humor doesn't get no respect." It's rare to find a reflective discussion on the relationship between Christianity and humor.[1] So why do Christian thinkers have so little interest in a topic that plays a central role in people's lives? After all, theologians stick their noses into just

---

[1]A few sources that deal with this topic are Harvey Cox, *The Feast of Fools: A Theological Essay on Festivity and Fantasy* (New York: Harper & Row, 1969); M. Conrad Hyers, ed., *Holy Laughter: Essays on Religion in the Comic Perspective* (New York: Seabury Press, 1969); James Martin, *Between Heaven and Mirth: Why Joy, Humor, and Laughter Are at the Heart of Spiritual Life* (New York: HarperOne, 2012); John Morreall, *Comedy, Tragedy, and Religion* (Albany: State University of New York Press, 1999); Susan Sparks, *Laugh Your Way to Grace: Reclaiming the Spiritual Power of Humor* (Woodstock, VT: SkyLight Paths, 2010).

about every other subject and take each of them pretty seriously. But when it comes to humor, we often listen for their take on the matter and hear only crickets, punctuated occasionally by negative comments before they again revert to silence.

FUNNY ISN'T THE OPPOSITE OF SERIOUS

> Mr. McCabe thinks that I am not serious but only funny, because Mr. McCabe thinks that funny is the opposite of serious. Funny is the opposite of not funny and nothing else.[2]

Perhaps the main reason Christian scholars haven't taken humor seriously is that they don't think that humor is serious, a view confirmed for many by the plethora of poop jokes available. Thus, they may see humor as "the competition," just another thing that vies for our attention and distracts from thinking earnestly about God. But I'm with Chesterton here. Funny and serious are not opposites. To joke about something requires that we deem it sufficiently important to search for the humor in it, and I will argue later in the book that even poop jokes may be more profound than we recognize. Moreover, we should also acknowledge that humor frequently draws us into the big questions of our existence. Think of all the jokes you know (but possibly can't tell some people) about love, death, God, sex, children, good and evil, and politics—"meaning of life" sorts of topics. In this way, humor certainly pays attention to questions of deep concern to theology, so why hasn't the attention (not to mention the affection) been mutual? The attitude that humor negates seriousness also lacks consistency. Other parts of our lives that we take seriously—family, friendships, work relationships, leisure, and church life—have room for laughter and are enriched by it. It seems that theology's lack of professional courtesy to humor relies on a deficient definition of seriousness.

---

[2]Gilbert K. Chesterton, *Heretics* (Grand Rapids: Christian Classics Ethereal Library, 2002), 72, www.ccel.org/ccel/chesterton/heretics.html.

Another obstacle that humor faces from Christians comes from a lopsided understanding of spirituality. Humor centers on our bodies, and often on its lowest features and functions. Spirituality, on the other hand, seems to be concerned with souls and spirits. Laughter is short-term and ephemeral, but the spiritual is about eternal life. Jokes and quips are usually specific to a situation, but our life with God transcends any single moment or event. Moreover, funny is enjoyable, and some Christians don't appear to find this compatible with being spiritual. Indeed, it may be that many Christians see humor as competition to their spiritual quests and don't appreciate it, somehow failing to note that *joy* is the root of *enjoyment* and is a word liberally spread throughout Scripture. Once again, I will argue that opposing humor and spirituality involves a flawed definition of spiritual development.

. . . WALK INTO A BAR

An airline pilot, a one-eyed Greek redhead, a giant, and an alligator walk into a bar.
  The bartender says, "What is this? Some kind of joke?"

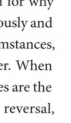

I don't want to shoot off too much of my ammo before we even get through the book's introduction, but let me lay a foundation for why Christians should view humor as a vehicle for taking faith seriously and pursuing spiritual growth and understanding. In normal circumstances, we anticipate that certain people will walk into a bar together. When these expectations are shaken up and worlds collide, good jokes are the result. Humor is about incongruity, surprise, misdirection, reversal, and other elements that shatter expectation. That's why we can find humor all around us. Whether it arises as a clash of generations, body and soul, good and evil, wife and husband, or in imagining what might happen if a one-eyed Greek redhead pulls up a barstool next to an alligator, funny occurs when worlds collide.

These sorts of juxtapositions occur on every page of the Bible. Heaven invades earth, humanity encounters God, and the future overlaps with the present. Our expectations are dashed when Saul the Super-Jew who persecutes the new Christian community becomes Paul the Apostle to the Gentiles (Gal 2:7) or an obscure shepherd kid, the youngest of Jesse's rather large brood of sons, becomes King of Israel (1 Sam 16:11-13). In our own lives, we feel the dialectic of being both saved and sinner, or heirs of the God of Heaven who also get stuck in freeway traffic. Perhaps there is no bigger cosmic collision than God becoming flesh. And if I started that story by saying that a poor unmarried couple, a group of shepherds, and some foreign astrologers walked into a stable together, it might remind you of a joke. It is precisely that: a glorious, beautiful joke that no one expected, and it brought salvation.

HUMOROUSLY

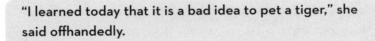

"I learned today that it is a bad idea to pet a tiger," she said offhandedly.

(My apologies, but good adverb jokes are hard to come by.)

The point of this book is not that we should scour Scripture looking for humor on every page, although there is a lot more there than we usually recognize.[3] Instead, the suggestion is that we should employ the structures and mechanisms of humor to gain insight into the Christian faith. Stated otherwise, the idea is that we think of Christianity, and ourselves, *humorously*. This is an "adverbial" approach to faith and humor. Adverbs, if I remember my junior high grammar correctly, describe actions and modify verbs; they talk about how something is done (and frequently end in -ly). The primary theme in this book, then,

---

[3]Some sources on humor in Scripture are Howard R. Macy, *Discovering Humor in the Bible: An Explorer's Guide* (Eugene, OR: Cascade, 2016); Elton Trueblood, *The Humor of Christ* (New York: Harper & Row, 1964); Steven C. Walker, *Illuminating Humor of the Bible* (Eugene, OR: Cascade, 2013).

it to meditate on what we might see in Scripture and in our faith when we look at them humorously.

It is hard to define *humor* itself. A dictionary definition such as "something that is or is designed to be comical or amusing"[4] hardly seems to capture the richness and variety of humor. Instead of attempting to define humor, it seems more helpful to focus on how it works. Humor builds on punch-line surprises, disruption of the conventional, reversal of expectation, juxtaposition of seeming incommensurate things, challenging boundaries, misinterpretation, redefinition of the familiar, satire, paradox, irony, and other related devices. If these elements are also part of the very fabric of the Christian story—and I'm convinced they are—then reading Scripture humorously holds the possibility of opening dimensions of the faith in new ways, seeing things from a fresh vantage point, and recognizing some spiritual blind spots. God defeats Israel's enemies with a woefully undermanned military force armed with band instruments (Judges 7), elevates Jacob the gimpy swindler to the role of Patriarch of the Chosen People, and adopts us as heirs of eternal life "while we were yet sinners" (Rom 5:8). Doesn't it seem possible that these incongruities and surprises share common ground with humor, and isn't the delight we should feel at the oddity of these stories akin to the delight we experience in a good joke?

The flip side of this adverbial methodology will provide a secondary motif within the book, in that I will raise the question of what it might mean to think about humor *theologically*. Jimmy Fallon's cue line to signal the beginning of his *Tonight Show* monologue is "Here's what people are talking about." If we listen carefully, we discover what those around us are talking about through their humor. Jokes about death, sex, gates of heaven judgment, money, politics, and marriage cue us in to the fact that ultimate issues are top of mind for people. Gallows humor and

---

[4]www.merriam-webster.com/dictionary/humor.

quips about aging and nonfunctional body parts expose human fears and provide glimmers of hope. Insecurities and a sense of impotence are often the undertones in sarcasm directed at the wealthy and powerful. Self-deprecating humor is often the only form of confession that we will hear from friends and neighbors. This list will grow as we move through the book, but suffice it to say here that humor is often the conduit by which we express our frustrations, anxiety, joys, loves, and opinions about life's biggest issues. Since these are obviously matters of theological concern, we ought to be theologically attuned to humor.

If the only tool you have is a hammer, everything starts to look like a nail.

The aim of these musings about humor's relationship to Christianity is not to create a happy-face church that is more fun than our usual offerings, an alternative to the comedy club without the two-drink minimum. Not to say that some congregations couldn't make things a tad more interesting. Some churches feel like a hostage situation in which they hope the captives will hang around long enough that Stockholm syndrome will kick in and they'll eventually join the cause. Instead, I view interpreting faith humorously as *a* way, one way, of thinking about who we are and who God is. I'm working hard to be sensitive to the tunnel vision that often accompanies the zeal of a new convert. Reading Christianity humorously has brought a freshness to my faith, and I'm excited about this. But it leads to the temptation to overstate the case and see humor even where it isn't.

The Christian faith has a broad array of valid forms of expression. Sermons, heartfelt conversation, devotional thoughts, and a range of other forms all have their place and are useful. Still, I'm also convinced that one of the most potent ways of expressing, understanding, and deepening faith is woefully underutilized. Too often, humor has been sidelined, even discouraged, as a means of exploring, learning about, or growing in faith. However, Ecclesiastes tells us there is "a time to weep, and a time to laugh" (Eccles 3:4). It seems that many Christians are overdue on finding a time to laugh, and I am convinced that our life in God's presence warrants a lot more laughter than we've imagined.

DISSECTING FROGS

Humor can be dissected, as a frog can, but the thing dies in the process and the innards are discouraging to any but the purely scientific mind.[5]

For most of its history, philosophy, like theology, has refused to give humor much professional courtesy. In recent years, however, a flurry of philosophy-of-humor books has emerged.[6] Some of that research lies beneath the surface of this book, but a lot of this material has the tendency to kill all that is good about humor.[7] Unfortunately, this isn't uncommon when philosophers get hold of an interesting topic—and this should stand as a warning about reading anything on the philosophy of sex.

Given the dangers of death by overanalysis, this book has rather modest goals. The intent is to raise an overlooked and underappreciated topic, but not in a way comes close to what you might call a robust "theology of humor." It will deal with some traditional theological topics—theological anthropology, incarnation, death and resurrection, ecclesiology, general revelation, and eschatology—but I don't pretend to give any of these subjects a thorough treatment and will stay away from most of the tricky and nuanced questions that arise in each area. I have enough on my hands just trying to make the case for the value of humor and laughter in our theological inquiries. This is nothing

---

[5]E. B. White and Katharine S. White, preface to *A Subtreasury of American Humor* (New York: Coward-McCann, 1941), xvii.

[6]A good place to start with philosophy and humor is John Morreall, *Comic Relief: A Comprehensive Philosophy of Humor* (Malden, MA: Wiley-Blackwell, 2009), and Simon Critchley, *On Humour* (New York: Routledge, 2002). Robert R. Provine, *Laughter: A Scientific Investigation* (New York: Viking Press, 2000), as the subtitle says, offers a scientific approach.

[7]Wood suggests that listening to a lecture on comedy is a bit like being slapped in the face with a recipe for custard pie. Ralph C. Wood, *The Comedy of Redemption: Christian Faith and the Comic Vision in Four American Novelists* (Notre Dame, IN: University of Notre Dame Press, 1988), 3.

more than a series of meditations on thinking humorously about theology, thinking theologically about humor, and attempting to encourage a conversation that I believe will be valuable to faith.

If any book cries out for a unity between medium and message, it is this one. A book about theology and humor ought to include humor, and perhaps a little theology. Thus, I have endeavored to incorporate laughter into the process and to keep the tone light and, hopefully, entertaining enough that you don't even realize that you are reading theology.

A couple of things to be said about that. First, some will find the tone and format disrespectful and unserious precisely because it incorporates humor. There is nothing further from my intent; my deepest desire is to honor God and help others think clearly and differently about faith. But I also happen to think that one of the best ways to do that is to include joy and laughter, as I would if I were in a serious theological discussion with good friends. More importantly, I believe that good theological reasons exist for making laughter part of our considerations of Christianity. As Karl Barth states: "If you have heard the Easter message, you can no longer run around with a tragic face and lead the humorless existence of a man who has no hope. One thing still holds, and only this thing is really serious, that Jesus is the Victor."[8] We are resurrection people, and if elated laughter is not part of our faithful repertoire, I'm not sure we really get Easter.

Second, I need to acknowledge that although humans of every era enjoy humor, the forms differ over time, across culture, according to gender, and in relation to our moral and religious commitments. Humor is a matter of taste.[9] What one person will find incredibly funny

---

[8]Karl Barth, *Dogmatics in Outline*, trans. G. T. Thomson (New York: Harper & Row, 1959), 123.

[9]Benign-violation theory is one of the most popular explanations of what makes something funny. It states that a joke must violate our expectation of what should be and that this violation is benign. In slapstick, a slip and fall (violation of the expected) may be judged as funny if the person is not injured (benign outcome) but not if a leg is broken (not benign). Tickling is a violation of personal space, but is benign if done by a friend. Things are generally considered funnier as they approach "the line" that separates the benign from an actual violation. A joke cannot be too

8

will elicit yawns or bring offense to others. I have a high tolerance for humor that some find objectionable (and a low tolerance for those in perpetual search of anything that could be perceived as objectionable). Out of consideration for others (and a desire to have the book published), most of the time I have stayed on the safe side, but it has been painful. When the humor and subject matter does move toward the earthy and guy-humor side, it does so to make a theological point.

A final disclaimer is that I am neither a theologian nor a comedian. As far as theology goes, I am an amateur both in the professional sense and in the sense that an amateur is "one who does something for the love (*amour*) of it." I am a philosopher by trade, and philosophers are often quite hilarious, though rarely on purpose. Apparently, I was much funnier when my kids were young, but according to them, that ability faded long ago. The jokes and quips within the book have several sources. When I knowingly use material from a professional comedian, I give credit. Those who devote their skills to bring levity to our lives deserve no less. However, jokes often enter the public domain by retelling without attribution, and since joke details and vocabulary vary with repetition, it is quite possible that some have originated from professionals and do not receive due credit. My apologies if that has happened. The remaining materials are my own invention or have been drawn from my decades-long memory bank of humor, stories, and jokes shared by family and friends, and, of course, the internet.

"safe," or it isn't funny. However, personal taste must be considered because "the line" that separates the benign from the offensive lies in different places for different people. See A. Peter McGraw and Caleb Warren, "Benign Violations: Making Immoral Behavior Funny," *Psychological Science* 21, no. 8 (2010): 1142.

1

GOD HAS TO BE IN THERE SOMEWHERE

> When I die, I want to go quietly in my sleep like my grandpa. Not yelling and screaming like the other people in his car.

It's a bit dark, but I like this joke. It has the classic structure of a good one—setup and punch line. The setup line recognizes that we all fear encountering excruciating pain and prolonged suffering before death. Thus, it captures our attention, pulls us in, and makes us participants. Then the punch line comes; the unexpected is introduced and we end up in a very different place than what we initially anticipated. For some reason we like this. The surprise brings happiness and laughter.

I love humor, and I love God. So it's natural that I wanted these two objects of my affection to love each other. That didn't appear likely. Humor is fluffy; God is profound and holy. Theology is serious; jokes are silly—or so it seemed. Moreover, theology talks about all of life's big questions, but humor didn't seem to make theology's big-questions cut. I really wanted this relationship to work out, but two thousand years of theological reflection have mostly ignored humor as an area of interest. I began to fear that my desire to find connections between my faith and humor were just wishful thinking.

Still, I couldn't let it go. Maybe it's because I was convinced that if humor brought joy and hope (and it does), God must be in there somewhere. However, I think the main reason I suspected that humor and

11

God already had an intimate relationship was because humor is one of the main ways that I express love. I say "I love you" to my wife and kids frequently, but not always with the words themselves. More often, it comes across by telling a joke, watching funny YouTube videos with the kids, teasing, or doing goofy things calculated to elicit groans. And when I employ groan-inducing dad humor, my kids' response is sometimes "I hate you," which, when stated with a chuckle, really means "I love you." At least that's how I'm reading it.

If I said "I love you" directly to my friends, they would probably suspect that I recently had been diagnosed with Stage IV cancer. But I try to express my love for them with reports of the most recent offbeat news stories I ran across, funny occurrences in the classroom, mutually traded insults that morph into expressions of affection through the mystical prism of guy talk, and (again) jokes. I just couldn't bring myself to believe that one of the primary vehicles by which I communicate and receive love had nothing to do with God. Moreover, humor's "I love you" function presented a serious challenge to the charge that humor is too frivolous for service in the Christian life. If humor is a love delivery system for humans, it seemed likely that God just had to be in there somewhere and that we might discover a healthy dose of LOL in God. Even though I'm sure God is not nearly as awkward as I am about communicating love, I still didn't see why humor couldn't be one of the ways God expresses his love for us.

THEN IT HIT ME . . .

 I couldn't figure out why the baseball kept getting bigger and bigger. And then it hit me.

One "aha" moment kicked my interest in potential connections between theology and humor into a higher gear. It was the realization that what we generally consider the bottom feeder in the comedic pond—the pun—actually requires a highly complex intellectual capacity. Getting it requires the ability to rapidly flip through a Rolodex of different possible meanings for words and phrases and recognize the juxtaposition of two definitions. Without one of my highest mental processes, the so-called lowest form of humor fails to hit me in the funny bone. At the same time, the pun above is one that a second-grader of average intelligence could understand.

What happens when we move on to more sophisticated forms of humor? I tried a little experiment. I told the following joke to my shih tzu:

> After taking a bite of the forbidden fruit, Adam knew he had done wrong, felt shame, and covered himself with a fig leaf.
>
> Eve also felt shame, and she too covered herself with a fig leaf, and then went back into the forest to try on some magnolia greenery, a palm frond, and three varieties of mulberry leaves.

Tofu the shih tzu didn't get the joke. I then tried it out on a border collie since that breed is 130 levels higher on the canine intelligence index. Still nothing. Only humans get humor. As simple as it seems on the surface, the humor in this joke goes far beyond a canine's mental and cultural repertoire. It obviously requires language skills that dogs lack, but it also demands cultural and religious background knowledge, the capacity to comprehend the moral emotion of shame, and to place oneself into the mind-set of another who feels shame, an awareness of gender stereotypes— *"Adam, does this fig leaf make my butt look big?"*— and the consciousness that this joke nudges a line that imperfectly delineates funny from offensive. And yes, I do realize that some will be offended by this joke. My shih tzu didn't take offense at it, and it's not simply because he's a socially insensitive male. He's not human (but don't tell him), and humor is possessed by no species on this planet other than human beings.

Like humor, spiritual sensitivity is a human capacity. And spiritual awareness, like our comedic sensibilities, demands the intellectual, moral, social, and emotional horsepower supplied by our highest human capacities. In fact, the capacity to grasp the alternative world that humor requires is the same mental ability that allows us to envision a God who transcends the natural realm. If our loftiest and most complex abilities are gifts from God and are as essential to the life of faith as they are to the existence of humor, I couldn't help but conclude that God must be lurking somewhere in our comedic capacities. The precise nature of the connection was still a mystery to me. However, as I reflected further upon what humor does and how it works, it became increasingly mysterious to me why so few have seriously considered whether humor might be an important theological resource.

MYSTERY #1—DOES THE *IMAGO* GIGGLE?

Theology has a long history of attempting to pin down a precise definition for the phrase "the image of God" (or if you want to sound smart, the *imago Dei*). The one thing that seems clear from Scripture is that this *imago* is borne by human beings alone. Thus, the leading candidates for interpretations of the divine image include the inventory of uniquely human faculties: cognition, will, language, creativity, moral sensibility, intentional community, mutual relationality, and aesthetic capacity. Because these God-imaging abilities are at the heart of our humanity, Christians have thought for centuries about the connections between faith and image-of-God capacities such as reason, ethics, emotion, psychology, communication, and imagination. We have written thousands of "theology of" or "theology and" books on uniquely human endeavors such as music, art, culture, language, worship, politics, and economics. And so we should.

Here's the mystery. As we noted in the prior Adam and Eve joke, humor employs all the image-of-God capacities. Why then does it not occur to us to think carefully about humor in the context of faith? Is the ability to giggle part of the *imago*? Surely the first bearers of God's image had the ability to recognize and understand humor. It may also be that, in hindsight (there's a pun in there somewhere), they recognized that it was a bit odd that they were naked in the Garden and it was fruit that tempted them.

MYSTERY #2—INTEGRATING OUR HUMANITY

While critters lack the mental, moral, and spiritual functions that allow for humor, some primates have physical expressions and vocalizations that roughly parallel human smiles and laughter.[1] Higher primates have facial expressions that have similarities to a human smile when "being tickled" or greeting one another. This seems to excite those who, for reasons that escape me, revel in discovering factoids that appear to level off the differences between humans and animals. However, there is a huge difference between human and gorilla grins. Their "smiles" and laughter-like vocalizations are embedded in instincts of fight and flight. In contrast, our laughter is integrated across the full scope of our human capacities.

When I hear the quip *Cured ham? Apparently not, or I wouldn't be eating it,* the neurological activity that processes the language and recognizes incongruous ideas syncs up with facial muscles into a smile. Simultaneously, my emotional state brightens and I feel a sense of connection with the person who delivered the line. Laughter stimulates blood flow, reduces stress, and, if we reach the point of a full belly laugh, burns a few calories.[2] A line that may be mildly amusing if read from a website brings convulsions of the diaphragm in the hands of an expert

---

[1]"Tickled Apes Yield Laughter Clue," BBC News, June 4, 2009, http://news.bbc.co.uk/2/hi/science /nature/8083230.stm.

[2]Lawrence Robinson, Melinda Smith, and Jeanne Segal, "Laughter Is the Best Medicine: The Health Benefits of Humor and Laughter," Helpguide.org, www.helpguide.org/articles/mental -health/laughter-is-the-best-medicine.htm/.

who delivers it with just the right intonations, raises an eyebrow at the right time, or nails the timing of a punch line. Humor and the resulting laughter is a whole-person experience that integrates everything from my spiritual, moral, and intellectual capacities—*He who laughs last, thinks slowest*—right down to the optic nerve, cheek muscles, and my glandular system. The amazing thing is that all of this occurs with no negative side effects.

When Scripture tells us to love God with heart, soul, mind, and strength (Mk 12:30), the presence of the "and" rather than an "or" in this sequence strongly implies that this is not multiple choice. Loving God should engage every facet of our being—spiritual, emotional, physical—and bring each together in harmony, the same kind of harmony and integration we experience across our whole being in humor. Upon hearing the news that she carries the Savior in her womb, Mary sings, "My soul magnifies the Lord, and my spirit rejoices in God my Savior" (Lk 1:46-47). Do we believe she "magnifies" and "rejoices" with a scowl or a somber expression? Was she just laughing on the inside? Did her psychological outlook, adrenaline level, and pulse rate remain the same? Or does it seem more probable that then and throughout her pregnancy she smiled, and maybe even laughed aloud, every time she thought about the joy and oddness of what was happening? Did the world around her seem new and different? If humor brings the diverse dimensions of our being into congruence with each other, why should we not be interested in its potential implications for a faith that integrates our God-gifted capacities?

MYSTERY #3—THE QUEST FOR UNITY

 God warned his children, Adam and Eve, not to eat the forbidden fruit. Of course, they wanted to know why not, and God said, "Because I am your Creator and I said so!"

Minutes later, God saw them eating the fruit and confronted them: "Didn't I tell you not to eat that?"

"Uh-huh," Adam replied.

"Then why did you?"

"I dunno," Eve answered.

"She started it!" Adam said.

"Did not!"

"DID so!"

"DID NOT!"

Having had it with the two of them, God's punishment was that Adam and Eve should have children of their own. The pattern was set, and it remains to this day.

Have you ever read or heard a joke you couldn't wait to tell someone else? I ran across this one when my own kids were young, and I quickly (and probably obnoxiously) shared it with a number of my friends who were in a similar stage of child-rearing. We were able to laugh together about the challenges that come with raising kids, even when they are great kids. The humor unified us in the realization that we were in this together, and it paved the way to talk openly about the struggles and the joys of parenting.

Humor has magnetic properties. Out of twenty-three qualities one might seek in a potential mate, a BBC survey of more than two hundred thousand from a variety of nations found that males deemed humor as the third most desirable trait in potential partners, while females ranked it at the top of their list.[3] People who have a sense of humor are perceived as warm, caring, and above average in intelligence.[4] Those

---

[3]Richard A. Lippa, "The Preferred Traits of Mates in a Cross-National Study of Heterosexual and Homosexual Men and Women: An Examination of Biological and Cultural Influences," *Archives of Sexual Behavior* 36, no. 2 (April 2007): 109.

[4]There is a strong correlation between a sense of humor and intelligence. A study done on nationally known comedians showed that the mean IQ of males in this group was 138, while the mean for female comics was 126. Samuel S. Janus, Barbara E. Bess, and Beth R. Janus, "The Great Comediennes: Personality and Other Factors," *The Journal of Psychoanalysis* 38, no. 4 (December 1978): 368.

who laugh easily and bring laughter are judged to be more loving people. In fact, Robert Provine, a psychologist who specializes in laughter, found that we are thirty times more likely to laugh in social settings than when we're alone.[5] We like to laugh, and we especially like to laugh with others.

Humor draws us together and is often the lubricant that allows us to engage in conversation about difficult issues. The reason we enjoy a joke is because it gives life to something within us, and sharing it with another ideally seeks to stir something similar within them that creates an interpersonal bond. In a world where the walls that divide us theologically, culturally, politically, and otherwise seem to get higher and thicker, why doesn't it occur to us to investigate humor as a serious tool for removing deadly barriers and moving toward the unity God wants for Christians? If humor is a love language that brings people together and allows us to build bridges, might it be that we should speak of the God who is the source of love in that same language? If a sense of humor makes people more lovable, would not a God who is love and desires our love be lovable for this quality? If we find it easy to relate to those who laugh, is it so hard to believe that God, in God's own way, laughs?

MYSTERY #4—DID WE LOSE EASTER SOMEWHERE?

A grandmother was concerned that her granddaughter didn't understand the Christian significance of the holidays, so she asked the young girl some questions to see if those fears were justified.

"Honey, can you tell me what Thanksgiving is really about?"

"Nana, it's about saying thank you to the native people who helped the Pilgrims survive."

Concerned, Grandma pressed on. "And why do we celebrate Christmas?"

---

[5]Robert Provine, "Laughing, Tickling, and the Evolution of Speech and Self," *Current Directions in Psychological Science* 13, no. 6 (December 2004): 215.

The child responded, "It's to celebrate the birth of Santa."

Now quite worried, Grandma tried one more time. "What is Easter about?"

The little girl smiled and said, "That's easy. We're celebrating Jesus coming out of the tomb."

The older woman breathed a sigh of relief until her granddaughter finished her response. "And if he sees his shadow, we'll have six more weeks of winter."

If you want to talk about evil, suffering, injustice, oppression, and death, Christians have these topics well covered. We have grief classes and trauma recovery groups, rescue missions, food pantries, social justice organizations, and boxcars full of books that speak of all that is devastatingly wrong in the world, all through the lens of Christian faith. This is good, and I praise God for those who push back in these ways against the powers of darkness. They follow the same job description Jesus lays out for his own earthly ministry: "to bring good news to the poor . . . to proclaim release to the captives and recovery of sight for the blind, to let the oppressed go free" (Lk 4:18).

Our present age is a twisted version of Groundhog Day, with each new morning bringing echoes of the death and evil of Good Friday. Scripture seems to make it clear that if we fail to minister among those who experience life's darkness, we forfeit the right to call ourselves Jesus' disciples. Darkness is not the only reality though, and at the risk of sounding insensitive to those who endure the full force of suffering and marginalization, it is not the primary reality. We can only call Good Friday "good" by looking backward through the window of Easter resurrection.

If Easter redefines crucifixion Friday as Good Friday, it also reframes the suffering, mourning, and tears of that day so that elation, joy, and uncontrollable laughter are appropriate, and in a double sense. It is not just happiness at the reversal of the tragic, but the happy surprise that what seemed so final is not the last word after all. If this is true, shouldn't our ministries among those who hurt aim at the giddiness that is characteristic of wholeness and resurrection life? Shouldn't our spiritual life be infused with joy, laughter, and humor as reminders of the ultimate defeat of suffering and evil? Mockery is a dangerous form of laughter, but doesn't it seem appropriate to join the Easter chorus singing, "Where, O death, is your sting?" (1 Cor 15:55).

MYSTERY #5—ACCOUNTING FOR ALL THE POWER TOOLS

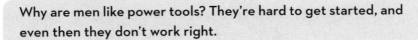

Why are men like power tools? They're hard to get started, and even then they don't work right.

God has invested many things in creation with great power. Money, sex, politics, and art all have the potency to achieve great things if used properly but are utterly destructive if misused. Christians have taken note, so they talk, write, and preach about how to harness these power tools for honoring God. Humor is also a power tool. It can be a potent device for drawing people together, healing, and giving freshness to life. It is often one of the few forms of power available to the powerless and is found throughout Scripture as a way for God's exiled and oppressed people to resist the principalities and powers and hold on to hope. But there are forms of laughter that destroy humans as well. Scorn and ridicule often belittle. Stereotype and caricature can depersonalize. If for no other reason than the fact that laughter can wound, Christians ought to give it deep thought.

Many Christians are familiar with the old question, Why should the devil have all the good music? although, in typical Christian fashion, we can't agree on who said it first. But it is a good question, no matter who came up with it. Take a look at the Amazon list of the top one hundred books in the category "Religious Humor." Tragically, virtually every book on the list uses humor to mock and denigrate faith and people of faith, and it is a powerful tool for doing so. It seems we are past due for a hard look at how we can harness the power of humor and laughter as a vehicle *for* faith. After all, Why should the devil have all the good laughter?

MYSTERY #6—WE LIKE TO LAUGH

As a kid, the first thing I would do while waiting in a medical office was to grab the *Reader's Digest* and read all the joke sections. I still do this as an adult, even though it seems that *Reader's Digest* is not as readily available in medical offices at the time in my life when doctor visits have become more frequent. While most of the things I used to enjoy as a kid don't hold much sparkle for me now, my love for humor has continued unabated throughout my life. From what I can tell, I'm not alone in this. Everyone likes to laugh. The capacity to giggle and guffaw emerges at an extremely early age and remains with us until death. The enjoyment of laughter spans every known group of people in every age. Even though humor takes different forms in different cultures, if a culture exists in which humor is absent, we haven't found it yet.

Humor is a constant and desirable dimension of human life, yet we almost never talk about its place in Christian life. Even if reading the *Reader's Digest* jokes did nothing more than momentarily distract us from the high-pitched scream of the dentist's drill in the next room, humor would have a valuable social function. But it does much more, bringing joy, health, friendship, and texture to the lives of people in all places and at all times. That should make us expectant that we could find the God who is the lover of all people in there somewhere, and it's a real mystery why the connection isn't automatic.

The point of examining these "mysteries" is to remind us that humor keeps showing up in the things we love and in the most profound things we do. This in itself seems to indicate that we should take humor seriously as a tool in living and expressing our faith. But I have become convinced that the connections between laughter and the Christian faith run even deeper. I think God is something of a jokester because the Christian story is full of the triggers and mechanisms that are at the core of humor: violating and challenging boundaries, reversal, incongruity, irony, tweaking the powerful, surprise, and other elements I will develop more in the next chapters. I know we aren't used to reading Scripture as humor or viewing God as a joke teller. If you don't buy this, you might want to check with Jonah—if you could find him in a better mood than he was right after his Ninevite revival meetings.

JONAH—WE'VE GOT A RUNNER

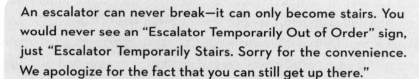

An escalator can never break—it can only become stairs. You would never see an "Escalator Temporarily Out of Order" sign, just "Escalator Temporarily Stairs. Sorry for the convenience. We apologize for the fact that you can still get up there."

MITCH HEDBERG

As we noted above, the basic structure of most jokes is the setup (an escalator can never break) and the punch line (it can only become stairs). Most of us are happy if we can pull this off and come away with the laugh. A real comedian isn't satisfied with this. The big payoff is when they follow up the joke with a "topper" (*You would never see an "Escalator Temporarily Out of Order" sign, just "Escalator Temporarily Stairs"*). Or they go for two (*"Sorry for the convenience"*), or even for three (*"We apologize for the fact that you can still get up there"*). Mitch Hedberg was a master at writing toppers, and even better at delivering them. However, the book of Jonah gives Hedberg a run for his money because it reads like a four-chapter joke series that stacks one topper on top of another.

"The word of the LORD came to Jonah son of Amittai: 'Go to the great city of Nineveh and preach against it, because its wickedness has come up before me.' But Jonah ran away from the LORD and headed for

22

Tarshish" (Jon 1:1-3 NIV). We are not even three verses deep in the book, and it is already pretty funny. Jonah is a missionary waiting for a call from God to preach. When it comes, he jumps on a ship sailing exactly the opposite direction instead of heading east to Nineveh. This catches us by surprise because we expect prophets to be the really spiritual people who will do exactly what God tells them, and Jonah dashes those expectations. A man called by God runs away from God's call. We also would think that a prophet has enough sense to know that hiding from God has a low success rate, yet running away from God is Jonah's intent. Apparently, HR should have vetted this prophet more carefully.

On board the ship, God sends a storm to try to get Jonah's attention. The prophet—the guy we expect to be keenly attuned to God's hints and whispers—is instead dead asleep in the bowels of the ship, totally unaware that his disobedience has put the lives of the entire crew at risk. When Jonah is finally apprised of the situation, he urges the sailors to chuck him overboard to save themselves. Unexpectedly, the crew attempts to save Jonah's life by rowing harder against the storm, even though they know he is the cause of all this turmoil. They act mercifully toward one who doesn't deserve it, which goes beyond duty and draws them into the category of moral excellence. When finally forced to toss Jonah overboard, the crew offers a sacrifice. Did you catch that? The pagans engage in an act of worship toward Jonah's God, while Jonah is disobediently running away from the same God—his God. A bit ironic, you think?

Once Jonah is in the roiling water, he is saved from certain death in the oddest way imaginable: he is swallowed by a large fish. After being trapped inside the fish's gut for three days, Jonah finally starts to come around and offers a pretty nifty prayer of thanksgiving to God, recognizing that without this intervention he would be a goner. After this attitude adjustment, the big fish "vomited Jonah onto dry land" (Jon 2:10 NIV), and when God calls him again to the mission field, "Jonah obeyed the word of the LORD and went to Nineveh" (Jon 3:3 NIV).

Once there, Jonah preaches what is perhaps the shortest evangelistic sermon ever recorded in history: "Forty more days and Nineveh will be overthrown" (Jon 3:4 NIV).[6] It probably isn't delivered too enthusiastically either. Whether it's because of the power of the words or because Jonah still reeks of half-digested carp and sardines, he gets the Ninevites' attention, and they respond in a big way. The whole city, from the king all the way down the social food chain, repents. In fact, repentance even goes down the literal food chain because the Ninevites cover themselves *and* their livestock in the sackcloth of repentance (Jon 3:8). When sorrow for sin reaches the sheep and goat level, it seems to indicate sincerity. God responds by sparing them all from destruction.

GOD DISAPPOINTS JONAH

At this point, we have a strange story with a happy conclusion, but it gets weird again. Apparently, Jonah doesn't like happy endings for Ninevites and has a beef with his boss: "I knew that you are a gracious and compassionate God, slow to anger and abounding in love, a God who relents from sending calamity" (Jon 4:2 NIV). Jonah is disappointed with God because God refused to go ballistic on one of the Hebrew peoples' archenemies. As a result, Jonah announces that he wants to die and goes outside the city limits to pout. Jonah's grumpiness is relieved for a while by the shade of a nice vine that God provides. But the next day, a divinely commissioned worm gnaws through the vine, exposing Jonah again to the sun and hot wind, and Jonah is back in full I-wish-I-could-just-die mode. You get less drama from a hormonal fourteen-year-old.

I think the story is hilarious. Nowhere in Jonah do things work out the way they're supposed to. The setup leads us to anticipate one thing, but the punch line whiplashes us in the opposite direction, and the punch line is followed up by one topper after another. The hated Ninevites and their bovines repent and experience salvation from God even

---

[6]In the Hebrew, this sermon is five words long.

though there is little reasonable expectation that they will be responsive to a terse and unimaginative sermon from a grumpy foreigner. The pagan Gentile sailors act morally and show proper spiritual sensitivity toward the God of the Hebrew people. The "hero" of the story is a moral and spiritual zero at almost every turn throughout the entire episode.

There is so much crazy funny material in here that that reading it with anything but a big smile on our face is evidence that we have misread it. However, to call it hilarious does not mean that it isn't a deeply serious story. Quite the opposite. It may be that we should tell some of our most profound stories in humor because it seems that is exactly what God does. Much more on that later. However, in our Jonah story, humor is the vehicle for serious truths that we need to hear repeatedly.

GOD'S WAYS

By trade, I am a philosopher, which means that my job description includes trying to find good answers to some of life's knottiest questions. One of the hazards of teaching philosophy in a Christian university is that one too often hears the phrase, "God's ways are not our ways" (compare Is 55:8-9). I don't disagree with this at all. In fact, this book assumes that God's ways are incongruous and shocking when compared to our ways and that humor results from this. However, when this phrase is used as an excuse to stop thinking, it induces the same nausea in me that caused Jonah's big fish to barf him out. I don't interpret "God's ways are not our ways" as an invitation to punt intellectually on first down when things are hard to understand. Instead of saying not to think, it tells us that we need to *think differently* if we want to have some clue about what God is up to. Surely God wants his people to have some idea about his ways.

I think humor helps us understand God's ways because these ways are full of unexpected punch lines. As we saw in the Jonah story, even though the Ninevites have built up a résumé that justifies God's wrath,

25

God backs off as soon as they say sorry. It may surprise us to learn that God loves the outsiders and that sometimes the people we think we are supposed to hate are more spiritually attuned to God than even the most inside of the insiders—people like Jonah. This is not "our way," and it clearly is not Jonah's way. But God's ways are gracious, and I'm pretty sure God wants us to know that. Wrapped up in the story is the message that God is not as impressed with Nineveh's military power and economic wallop as we are. Our way is to think, like Jonah, that the Ninevehs of our world hold our fate in their hands. God doesn't seem to agree and calls them out for judgment in the same way that God reminds Pharaoh, Babylon, and Rome that their power is paper-thin. Throughout time, humor has been a tool of political resistance, and God uses it throughout Scripture to subvert the Nivevehs of every era. I think God wants us to pick up on this.

Our way is to identify the folks with sparkling résumés and perfect SATs and GPAs. A recurring inside joke in the Bible is that God specializes in recruiting the least expected for big jobs and does some of his best work through people who are deeply flawed. Jonah is supposed to be the exemplar in the story, but he's such a jerk even a big, hungry fish barfs him out. So the story also recaps the motif that God forgives and uses big jerks. God does work in mysterious ways, but these are funny mysteries. If you don't see it, you aren't reading your Bible God's way, and you totally misread the Jonah story.

Once again, these are all punch lines we didn't see coming if our thoughts follow the typical expectations. However, if we have become accustomed to God's ways, it doesn't surprise us that God surprises us. Reversals, paradox, violations of the usual norms and expectations are par for the course. Indeed, they are reminders that God's ways seem weird if we take our usual view of the world as the norm. Bringing humor to the game helps us see the logic of God's ways and the irrationality of our normal ways of thinking. In short, the same tools that help us understand and enjoy humor seem closely related to the tools necessary to understand and enjoy God and God's good news.

CAPTAIN OBLIVIOUS

A 911 operator receives a frantic call from a woman who says, "My child just swallowed a needle."

The operator reassures her: "Don't worry, an ambulance has been dispatched and will be there in five minutes."

Almost immediately, the woman calls back and says, "Cancel the ambulance. I found another needle."

In addition to my conviction that humor helps us understand God's ways, I think it is an invaluable tool for understanding and properly loving ourselves. Let me illustrate by going back to Jonah. When God calls him at the beginning of the book, his response is about as bad as we could anticipate. Yet God saves him from death, gives his job back, and uses him to save 125,000 souls from destruction. After all that? Jonah. still. doesn't. get. it.

If I read this story and said, "Gee, Jonah should have been happy about the Ninevites' repentance," my kids' response would be, "Thank you for that amazing insight, Captain Obvious." This story is funny because Jonah is so completely oblivious to what is so completely obvious to every reader. Moreover, it's not just a state of oblivion that makes something funny. For example, the joke beginning this section wouldn't have been as funny if the mother had called back and said, "Cancel the ambulance. I found a nickel." She would still be clueless, but the joke loses steam because it is hard to see any connection between what she planned to do with the needle and the nickel.[7]

---

[7]Roberts refers to this as "appropriate impropriety." If the richest woman in the county would live to be the oldest person in her county, we would not find this ironic because wealth and longevity are not directly related. However, if she wins the lottery, it is ironic since winning the lottery and wealth are related. Robert C. Roberts, "Humor and the Virtues," *Inquiry* 31 (June 1988): 130.

Jonah's story is funny precisely because he is oblivious to what any God-follower absolutely should have known and celebrated. That a prophet ought to celebrate repentance and redemption falls squarely in the Captain Obvious category. However, instead of running this story through humor's filter, we go judgmental on Jonah. We're disappointed that Jonah didn't celebrate the fact that the Ninevites were spared from destruction. In fact, it even seems right to be angry with him. However, in both of these responses, we distance ourselves from Jonah and hold him at arm's length.

The danger in these responses is that we don't see ourselves in the story. Perhaps that distance is why Jesus had to tell the Jonah story again, this time in a parable about a lost son headed for destruction who is welcomed home by a forgiving dad but resented by an older brother who doesn't embrace his own dad's values.

I DIDN'T SEE THAT ONE COMING

(Behold, I stand at the door and) "Knock, knock."
"Who's there?"
"Jesus."
"Jesus, who?"
"I guess we all know who's going to hell, now."

Knock-knock jokes are usually pretty innocuous because they are usually just silly. ("*Knock, knock.*" "*Who's there?*" "*Wire.*" "*Wire who?*" "*Wire you asking?*" "*I just told you.*"—Just in case you needed evidence of this genre's silliness.) However, this Jesus knock-knock joke has some kick to it because instead of getting the anticipated silly answer, it pulls us in and puts us on the spot—rather unpleasantly so. We don't see it coming. We would like the prodigal son story to stop while it has the Disney-type ending. The lost son has come to his senses and the loving father welcomes him home. To be honest, the last part about the older brother is a bit of a buzzkill.

The prodigal son seems like a variation of the Jonah joke because it has the same punch line. The older brother who should know better just doesn't get it. Maybe if we could read this in the form of a joke, the punch line would land a little closer to home. From a detached perspective, we condemn the older brother. He's been there all the time. He knows the family "business" and the values it's built on. Instead of joining the party, he sulks. Just like Jonah. And like Jonah, he angers and disappoints us. But humor requires participation; we have to see ourselves in the characters. Through the eyes of humor, the setup puts us in the role of the older brother. We expect that he will be the star because he has stayed home and fulfilled his duty to his father. Then there is the reversal, and our engagement leaves us vulnerable. We now discover that we are Jonah and the prodigal's older brother and, at least at that moment, we're more lost than a bunch of Ninevites who "cannot tell their right hand from their left" (Jon 4:11 NIV) or a wayward young man who has not yet come to his senses and is still competing with pigs for lunch. We never saw that coming.

The ever-present temptation of the Christian life is to treat it like a spectator sport, where we call fouls and keep score from the sidelines. Faith doesn't work that way; neither does humor. Faith and humor have an element of danger because they only benefit us when we become vulnerable. They both subject us to judgment by telling us the truth about ourselves. In that sense, in both Jonah and the parable of the prodigal son and his clueless older brother, the joke is on us. Our failure to understand and love God's way is revealed to us, but the other side of this is that God's joke is not just *on* us. It is God's joke *for* us. Unexpectedly, it reminds us that we can become the redeemed Ninevite or a forgiven prodigal at the center of a celebratory feast featuring fatted calf as the main entrée.

Our faith demands a necessary and precarious balance of judgment and grace, and I think humor helps us with this. Good laughter does not let us off the hook with sin, because it acknowledges the utter stupidity of our actions. When done well, laughter is a form of showing disappointment and even anger at ourselves. When we laugh because of the freedom of redemption, it must be conditioned by a recognition that judgment has exposed us for who we too often are. However, laughing at the absurdity of our faults needs to be conditioned by our recognition that stupidity and rebellion can be reversed and forgiven. As the old saying states it, confession without repentance is just bragging. Without the combination of confession and turning around, we fall into the trap of cheap grace or suffocating guilt, and we are quite susceptible to both.

Because we are so spiritually dense, God has to sneak up and surprise us, but the joke is for us. This is the best part of the good news. While the truth about our life is often painful, the surprise of God's grace is that it benefits us. Thus, the prodigal's dad says, "we had to celebrate and be glad, because this brother of yours was dead and is alive again; he was lost and is found" (Lk 15:32 NIV). Joyful laughter in the presence of redemption is mandatory, not optional. God welcomes the wayward prodigal and the Ninevite home because God is for us—all of us.

2

YOU MAY NOT HAVE A SENSE OF HUMOR, BUT YOU ARE FUNNY

Years ago, I picked up my son, Zack, then four years old, from preschool. After we were both buckled in, I asked him about a particular classmate. "Do you play much with him at school?"

Zack said, "Not really. He cries too much."

I explained that his classmate probably cried a lot because his father had recently died in a car accident, and I suggested that it might be good to include him in things even though that might be hard.

After a short period of car-seat contemplation, Zack said, "I think Jesus would want me to be friends with him."

There was another moment of silence as I tried to determine whether fatherly wisdom was best displayed by affirming this priceless response or if any further statement would simply blunt its profundity.

Before I could make up my mind, Zack's voice from the back seat broke the silence. "My butt itches."

One reason I find humor so helpful in understanding ourselves is that our existence is magnificently paradoxical. If we were not yet familiar with our species, imagining a being who could glimpse the face of God and belch at the same time is a combination that might seem too incongruous to believe. The capacity to write or speak of love, beauty, or God with profound insight while wearing an "I'm with stupid" tank top, emitting unpleasant aromas, and eating microwaved pork rinds seems utterly incompatible. The sorts of diseases or accidents that will end our life are the same maladies and ills that kill donkeys. At the same time, the vast majority of humans believe that we will live after our physical demise. We can devote one hour to deep meditation on God's grace and mercy and follow it up by amusing ourselves with Bubble Wrap or TV, its visual equivalent, for the next hour, or six. We can endeavor to follow the example of the Son of God by loving sacrificially, and then we're thrown off track by itchy butt cheeks.

Humans do stuff like this, we know it, and the incongruity of it all is both jarring and funny. The fact that a human—God's own image—contains dirt (Gen 2:7) as a primary ingredient seems almost unthinkable, but humor thinks about it all the time, even if not consciously so. In fact, the Latin for dirt—*humus*—is only a short step from *human*. This all occurs because humor recognizes the tension of our physical and godlike dimensions. We know ourselves as both "a little lower than the angels" (Ps 8:5 NIV) but a single notch higher than aardvarks. We are, to delicately paraphrase Ernest Becker's definition of our species, gods that defecate.[1] Because we are aware that we are more than simply the sum of our biological functions and malfunctions, we find it odd that such physical activities intrude so frequently upon our life. The fact that humans pray, create art, build and launch spacecraft into the heavens, ponder the nature of justice, sacrifice for others, discern beauty in a sunset, and care about those who have suffered crushing loss makes it comical that we get the hiccups in the midst of these activities.

---

[1]Ernest Becker, *The Denial of Death* (New York: Free Press, 1997), 58.

> Kids in the back seat cause accidents. Accidents in the back seat cause kids.

> That little tingling feeling you get when you fall in love? That is caused by the last ounce of common sense leaving your body.

The paradoxical combination of high and low, animal and exalted, is present even in our most profound capacity—the capacity to love. On one end of the spectrum is *eros*, the erotic desire for the here today, gone tomorrow. The shelf life of *eros* may last only as long as a hormonal surge, yet those hormonal moments often produce the children we love so intensely that we would sacrifice our life for them, or at least sacrifice untold wealth to procure braces, violin lessons, food, and all the other expenses that come with parenthood. While *eros* seems a world away from *agape*, the love that characterizes God's embrace, they never are completely separate. If seen through Christian eyes, the crudest expressions of erotic yearning contain a cry for fulfillment and completion, a hunger for an intimacy that is pure and durable. I'm not sure what word you find most helpful in describing this desire for perfect love, but *salvation* comes to mind for me. If nothing else, it should strike us as surprising that English-language speakers employ the same word—*love*—to describe both our hankering for ice cream and our relationship with God.

I'm not trying to argue that our hybrid "creature in the Creator's image" existence is the source of all humor. However, it is hard to ignore how prevalent hybridity is to humor, whether it is found in when two definitions of the same word butt up against each other (*The dispenser said "crushed ice," but it seemed only mildly disappointed when it came out*); when two words that seem to be contraries are paired in an oxymoron (*scripted spontaneity* or *slumber party*); or in the juxtaposition of two images in a humorous analogy (*Camping: spending a lot of money to live like a homeless person*). Even the particulars of our existence are also ambiguous. I'm a Kansas farm boy from blue-collar roots teaching philosophy in Los Angeles (*Hegel is so messed up that there ain't enough baling wire to fix him*). My kids are Korean and Chinese, raised by two Caucasian parents. This generates a lot of jokes around our dinner table, but none of them are safe enough to use here. It's not just my family. We all have our "hyphenated" lives in which the tension between more than one dimension of our being offers a fertile seedbed for humor. However, behind it all, the meta-joke of human existence is the juxtaposition of our shared soul–body life.

FLUFFY ISN'T FUNNY

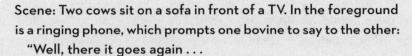

Scene: Two cows sit on a sofa in front of a TV. In the foreground is a ringing phone, which prompts one bovine to say to the other:
    "Well, there it goes again . . .
    And here we sit without opposable thumbs."

THE FAR SIDE

Every truly cultured person has a favorite *The Far Side* comic strip. This is one of mine. A large part of the humor in this panel emerges from our awareness that the absence of opposable thumbs is the tip of the iceberg when it comes to the impossibility of imagining actual bovines engaged in a phone call, watching TV from the comfort of their sofa, or comprehending the humor in this comic. What makes this even funnier is that many of the physical capacities of cattle, and of other animals, far surpass those of humans.

My dad had a cow herd for several years, and we would make routine trips to the pasture during calving season to check for newborns. If a newborn calf was not on its feet a few minutes after birth, we knew it was in trouble. By contrast, we don't look at a human baby born two hours prior and fret that he is not yet mobile. In fact, humans are so dependent for their survival on the older members of their species for such an extended portion of their lives that we aren't surprised to find them still living in their parents' basement at the age of twenty-eight. In the meantime, a healthy calf will be frolicking about the pasture on day two, albeit with frequent milk stops for a few months. Thus, the relative frailty of our own physical bodies and absence of basic survival skills when compared to those possessed by critters simply heightens the strangeness of our use of the body to play pianos, kneel in prayer, build skyscrapers, plant gardens, or treat our bovines for parasites. I think C. S. Lewis gets it right here: "Until some theory has sophisticated them, every man, woman and child in the world knows this. The fact that we have bodies is the oldest joke there is."[2]

In reality, *Homo sapiens* is the only animal species that is truly humorous because we alone experience an earthly–heavenly dichotomy. Whenever we find animals funny, it is because we impose human attributes or expectations on them. This sort of projection is natural because many of our limbs, organs, drives, and even our diets are similar. However, even though both my dog and I show up in the kitchen immediately upon hearing the microwave timer ding, he doesn't ponder whether it is morally or relationally insensitive that we are about to eat my son's leftovers. Nor does he pause to thank God for the vittles. When you view your favorite YouTube cat video, you are simply watching Fluffy be a cat. Fluffy is not funny, and she does not spend hours laughing at funny human YouTube videos. She may have trained you so that you reward her with treats or belly rubs every time she behaves in a particular way that appeals to *your* sense of humor. But properly speaking, Fluffy is not a humorous animal. Tigers and box turtles do not laugh at her. Fluffy is only funny *to us*.

---

[2]C. S. Lewis, *The Four Loves* (New York: Harcourt, 1960), 141. In this same location, Lewis speaks approvingly of St. Francis of Assisi's tendency to refer to his body as "Brother Ass": "Ass is exquisitely right because no one in his senses can either revere or hate a donkey. It is a useful, sturdy, lazy, obstinate, patient, lovable and infuriating beast; deserving now the stick and now a carrot; both pathetically and absurdly beautiful. So the body. There's no living with it till we recognize that one of its functions in our lives is to play the part of buffoon."

NATURALISM AS AN ANTI-HUMOR MOVEMENT

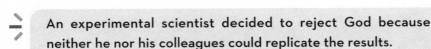

An experimental scientist decided to reject God because neither he nor his colleagues could replicate the results.

The fact that animals are not funny is one of the reasons I find a rather common tendency of our age to reduce the human being to purely animal status to be anti-humor, tragic, and heretical. I'll refer to this reductionistic worldview as naturalism since it rejects the existence of anything supernatural and accepts only the tangible world and its measurable forces as real. Thus, for the naturalist it would be true that gravity, carbon, water, bricks, rhinos, and electricity make the reality cut, but God and souls don't. In its attempt to get to the deepest knowledge of human nature, naturalism must abandon theology and even psychology, at least in its classical sense, since psychology literally means the study of the *psyche,* or "soul."

For the naturalist, belief in anything other than the physical is illusion or lunacy. This implies that our only access to true knowledge of the human being comes through physics, biology, chemistry, and similar disciplines. The human being is nothing more than a highly complex animal whose every activity, at least in principle, can be explained by physical "stuff" and the laws that govern the interactions of this stuff.

Although naturalism rejects any notion of God or gods, it is similar to a religious worldview in that it assigns to us a moral responsibility to believe the truth and argues that willful belief in ideas that rely on a supernatural explanation is a serious ethical failure. Those who reject its definition of the "real world" are viewed as unsophisticated rubes or mouth-breathing Luddites who want to drag the world back to a pre-scientific and superstitious past. Thus, by eliminating the "other world" and nonscientific means of knowing, naturalism erases the very origin of humor itself. As a result, naturalism's universe is itself a sick joke. In those many moments when the material realm seems to come into contact with the supernatural, naturalism declares that the latter is but an illusion. And naturalists consider illusions immoral and unfunny.

> Amy Farrah Fowler: Sheldon, there's something else I've been wanting to say, but before I do, I just . . . I want you to know that you don't have to say it back. I know you're not ready, and I don't want you to say it just because social convention dictates . . .
> Sheldon Cooper: I love you too.
> Amy: You said it.
> Sheldon: There's no denying I have feelings for you that can't be explained in any other way. I briefly considered that I had a brain parasite. But that seems even more far-fetched. The only conclusion was love.
>
> **THE BIG BANG THEORY**

Sheldon Cooper and his three fellow scientists on *The Big Bang Theory* are completely at home in quantum physics but are flummoxed by everyday life. Sheldon still can't drive a car—in *Los Angeles*, for heaven's sake. Allowing those of us who are scientifically incompetent to laugh at the inability of geniuses to navigate most mundane tasks has been a successful comedic formula for the series. However, their ineptitudes are not limited to obtaining a driver's license, sports, or wardrobe selection, although the latter is painfully obvious. Like so many sitcoms, much of the show's humor involves sex or, given the social awkwardness of the nerdy characters, their inability to procure sexual partners. Indeed, one of the main characters, Koothrappali, is so relationally incompetent that, for the first few seasons, he was incapable of speaking when a female was present unless he was drunk.

As *Big Bang* has evolved in more recent seasons, however, the scientists increasingly discover that they crave more than just sex. They desire an intimacy that cannot operate except within a moral framework, and neither intimacy nor morality is reducible to any of the tools available to them as scientists. They recognize that brain parasites and love are both potential causes for odd behavior. But even Sheldon Cooper, the character most resistant to extra-scientific explanations, has to admit that any attempt to reduce love to a mere physical cause is too "far-fetched."

Thousands of books have outlined the difficulties of materialistic explanations for human behavior and thought. How do we make sense of morality in beings who consist of amoral atoms? Why would beings governed by so-called selfish genes develop altruism? If human beings are animals guided by predatory instincts, why would we conclude that we ought to love both neighbor and enemy? If we are collections of particles and energies governed by ironclad rules of causation, how does freedom of choice arise in us? Or, if you are Sheldon Cooper, the question is why we can love another person if humans are nothing more than large skin bags containing a complex chemistry set.

Some people believe that naturalism has adequate responses to these questions, but I think this conclusion requires far too much faith (ironic since naturalists scoff at faith). The evidence from so many directions points to the conclusion that some supernatural reality exists and that we participate in it in some way. Perhaps I'm most convinced of this by this simple but persistent observation: we are funny creatures, the sorts of beings whose humor affirms and embraces our physical bodies and finds it quite odd that some other sort of something, a reality that cannot be reduced to chemicals and quarks, keeps intruding on it.

The problem for the naturalist's desire to reduce everything to chemical and biological functions is that pigs and petunias can't stop being pigs and petunias. As purely biological entities, they are what they are. Human beings, however, can remain biologically human and simultaneously lose their humanity. This is possible only because "human" is not only, or even primarily, a biological category. It is a moral and spiritual designation, a statement about what we ought to be. There is no ought to be for hogs, but there is no humanity, and no humor, apart from it. In this sense, humans are *sui generis*, while pigs are simply sooey generis.

GNOSTICISM—AN EQUAL AND OPPOSITE ANTI-HUMOR MOVEMENT

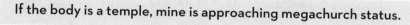

If the body is a temple, mine is approaching megachurch status.

Lest Christians start feeling too smug about avoiding naturalism's pitfalls, many of us fall prey to an anti-humor movement on the other end of the spectrum. We really ought to know better because it was the first big heresy in Christian history: gnosticism.[3] As I use it here, gnosticism designates any belief that refuses to recognize the physical as God-given, good, or real. For gnostics, bodies—even those not yet of mega-girth—are a problem.

Gnosticism gets off on the right foot by recognizing the dichotomous nature of our existence. For example, a prominent form of gnosticism (as just defined), Plato's philosophy is built around a dualism of body and soul. For him, the body is a physical shell dominated by fleeting sensory demands and lusts. The soul, by contrast, is a nonphysical reality, the seat of our recognition of the good, perfect, and divine. This hybrid existence is tragic rather than humorous, and our ultimate hope is that the soul, which Plato sees as the real me, is granted parole from its biological life sentence in the prison of the body so that it can enjoy eternity in the ethereal, changeless realm of perfection.

Because Plato gave an intellectual expression to the spiritual dimension of human existence, Christians throughout the centuries have had a bit of a love affair with him, and I can't help but think that this is

---

[3]As it is technically employed, Gnosticism refers to a family of religious philosophies built around cosmic and anthropological dualisms and a search for salvation that requires that we acquire esoteric knowledge. Under this definition, it is improper to lump Plato into this category. However, my broader and looser usage here is specified in the text that follows.

one of the main reasons Christians have tended to view humor with a jaundiced eye. The tension between the soulish and physical dimensions generates true humor and joy if and only if it is a conversation of one good with another. However, if the physical is incapable of goodness and salvation and cannot be comprehended as "a temple of the Holy Spirit" (1 Cor 6:19), our body's interactions with the soulish aspects of our life must be considered a form of warfare. Given this, if gnosticism sees the interactions of our dichotomous nature as a joke, it can be seen only as a sick joke that we should pray will end quickly.

Elsie was in her last hours of earthly life and, although conscious and clearheaded, had lost her ability to speak. Pastor John came by and sang Elsie's favorite hymn for her, thanked her for her faithful service to the congregation, and assured her that she would soon be in the presence of God. Elsie smiled and nodded, indicating affirmation of his words.

As Pastor John prepared to say a final prayer and continue his visitation rounds, Elsie became agitated, started to lose color, and her breathing became erratic. She signaled for a pencil and a scrap of paper, hurriedly scribbled a few words, and handed it to the pastor, who prayed her into eternity as she took her last breath.

A few days later at her funeral, Pastor John said, "Sister Elsie was fading fast, and I didn't have a chance at the moment to read her final words, but I thought it would be appropriate if we all heard them together." Reaching into his coat pocket, he unfolded the paper scrap and read, "Please move your foot. You're standing on my oxygen tube."

As with naturalism, my interest is not in offering an extended argument against a gnostic worldview. Instead, I simply observe that although modern gnostics may speak as if embodiment in this world is something we should desire to escape, they don't really act like this most of the time. Even Sister Elsie, confident that she will see her Savior's face in the resurrection, will still grab the doorknob on this side of the heaven's gates and hang on as long as possible. Moreover, perhaps it shouldn't go without notice that every time we hear a prayer request for physical restoration (a category that, by my informal reckoning, constitutes about 80 percent of prayer requests), we affirm our physical being.

I am reasonably certain that severing the bond between soul and body is what allows Christian gnostics to express disdain for laughter and physical pleasure while at the same time speaking frequently and positively, as Scripture does, about joy. For them, joy is the domain of our soul, an inward sense of goodness and well-being, while laughter is bodily. But experience seems to indicate that these worlds, while different, are inseparable. I find joy in the presence of my daughter, but this joy is enhanced by the warmth of her good-night hug. The confidence in my wife's loyalty through struggles gives rise to internal happiness, but a reassuring touch on the shoulder increases my *rejoicing* (a form of the word *joy* again). Reveling in a stimulating summer-evening conversation with friends on the deck brings a wonderful sense of inner connection. Having that conversation while *enjoying* (another form of the word) a perfectly or even imperfectly grilled steak? Priceless. My soul's joy is heightened, not diminished or contradicted, by the body's participation. This signals the goodness embedded in bodily being. Like all of us, Sister Elsie needs prayer and songs of worship. God made us that way. We, like Sister Elsie, also need the sort of stuff that shows up on the periodic table of elements; stuff like oxygen. That, too, was God's idea. In so many ways, we look like one big category mistake in which the holy and transcendent is comingled with carbon and blood that requires oxygenation. However, the fact that God visits our planet and takes on a meat body indicates that the physical (as well as the soulish) is redeemable.

Christian theology makes two things very clear: First, tangible creation, as an intentional act of a good God, is itself good. If you don't believe this, God said so here: Genesis 1:4; here: Genesis 1:10; here: Genesis 1:12; here: Genesis 1:18; here: Genesis 1:21; here: Genesis 1:25; and here: Genesis 1:31 (with "very" modifying the last "good," just in case you thought God wasn't really serious the first six times he said it). Second, Scripture is clear that all of creation is fallen. That applies to every aspect of our being, from our bodies to our soulish capacities such as reason, relationality, will, and moral sensibility. If you take away either of these two facets of us, you end up with something very different from Christianity.

In contrast, gnosticism does not teach the fall of a good creation. Gnostics *equate* embodied life on this physical planet with the fall. To be a material being in a material creation is to be fallen. Thus, gnostics cannot look back to "In the beginning God created the heavens and the earth" (Gen 1:1 NIV) or forward to "Then I saw a new heaven and a new earth" (Rev 21:1) to pick up cues of what salvation looks like. And when gnostically inclined Christians recite the creeds, it must seem quite odd to confess the resurrection of the body.

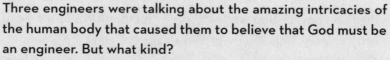

Three engineers were talking about the amazing intricacies of the human body that caused them to believe that God must be an engineer. But what kind?

One said God must be a structural engineer. Just look at the amazing framework provided by our bones, cartilage, tendons, and ligaments.

The second said that it seemed like God was more like an electrical engineer. After all, the circuitry of the brain, spinal cord, and nervous system looked like an electrical marvel.

The third said, "I'm convinced that God must be a civil engineer."

The other two were puzzled, but he explained: "Who but a civil engineer would run our primary sewage systems through a major recreational area?"

If you need a metaphor for the oddness of our hybrid existence and thus an argument against both naturalism and gnosticism, you can't do better than genitalia. Let's be honest. Our nether regions are the center both of our most unpleasant excretions as well as the most profound expressions of marital love and commitment. In a mysterious way, genitalia are seductively beautiful and, if you stop and think about it (although most people aren't doing much thinking when they are looking at genitalia), just plain goofy looking. It is hard to imagine a more animal activity than sexual intercourse, but that doesn't negate the fact that, properly understood (even if not properly executed), sex is simultaneously holy and sacramental, the physical expression of a relationship that should remind us of Christ's love for the church.

We have more euphemisms for genitalia than perhaps any other set of nouns in our language. Might this verbal veiling be a reminder that, while they are indeed a primary part of the human sewage system, genitals are also the closest analog of the holy of holies to be found on a body identified by God as his temple? We seem to know this intuitively. When Adam and Eve covered themselves with fig leaves in shame after disobeying God, Scripture doesn't specify what parts were hidden. Yet we already know that the first parents were not concealing their elbows and necks. Artist renderings all have the leaves strategically placed over the "naughty bits."

Christians have too often taken the gnostic route by denying or seeking to squelch sexual desire, embarrassed that something so closely related to the physical could be so doggoned pleasurable. However, the attitudes of most today tend toward naturalism's animalistic sexuality, in which the sole purpose is physical pleasure, which is nature's trick to get us to reproduce. At some point, however, such individuals have to be surprised that they can't seem to disconnect sex from moral and spiritual categories. Our journeys to the fun zone mysteriously cause us to think about words like *fidelity, betrayal, guilt,* and *love.* These intrinsic connections make more sense, however, if we recall that, alongside sex, the two other human experiences we are most likely to link with ecstasy (literally, "standing outside one's self") are music and worship. All three have a physical component that cannot be eradicated, but for those who have eyes to see, they reveal something transcendent about us that cannot be reduced to hormonal surges.

> **No one who has ever said that laughter is the best medicine had diarrhea at the time.**

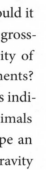

Since I've skated onto the thin ice by talking about sex, let's linger there for a while and have a conversation about poop humor. Should it surprise us that early adolescence, the zenith of our attraction to gross-out humor, coincides precisely with the time when the majority of human beings make their most significant religious commitments? Humor that features poop, barf, flatulence, pube, and armpit jokes indicates the struggle of coming to terms with the fact that we are animals at the same time we fall in love for the first time, begin to shape an identity independent of our parents, and make choices of such gravity that they may get us thirty days in jail rather than just thirty minutes of time-out in our naughty chair—all activities that set us apart from animals. In fact, the oldest joke we know of is a tenth-century BCE Sumerian joke about wives farting while on their husbands' laps.[4] The humor we find in our most animal operations emerges because it seems incongruous with our capacity to pray, write music, and debate politics. In view of these transcendent behaviors, secretions and bodily fluids make it impossible not to feel in some deep way that worlds are colliding.

One of the reasons sex and gross-out humor is so prevalent is that precisely at this point do we find our godlikeness and animal qualities

---

[4]If you really must know, the joke is: "Something which has never occurred since time immemorial; a young woman did not fart in her husband's lap." See "Flatulence Joke Is World's Oldest," *BBC News*, August 1, 2008, http://news.bbc.co.uk/2/hi/7536918.stm.

in closest proximity. We have wandered close to the forbidden, but at the same time, we stand on the outskirts of heaven. Thus, it may be a bit of a stretch, but I can't quite shake the idea that our humor about sex organs, vomit, body odor, and mucus is more than a reminder that we inhabit two worlds simultaneously. It also seems to be a soft apologetic, the echo of an argument for God's existence. If we are nothing but animals, conscious only of the natural dimension, copulation and urination are simply brute facts with no moral, economic, political, social, or spiritual implications. Not so with *Homo sapiens*. Without our capacity for the spiritual, we would never find bodily fluids funny— or yucky, for that matter.

If we have ears to hear, the fact that we snicker at boogers and poop signals that we know we are not ultimately defined by or limited to such physical functions and that sweaty people also inhabit a sacred dimension. We know that we are animals, but the only way we can know this is because we are more than mere animals. When we find that the temporary physical pleasure of sex cannot be successfully isolated from a for-as-long-as-you-both-shall-live type of love and caring, I just have to believe that the humor evoked in this clash of two worlds whispers hints of a good God's existence. We don't always want to hear it, but our humor indicates that we can't not know it.

REAL WORLD AND REAL ME

I'm not sure why they call it "reality TV" when there is nothing real about any of it. We don't want reality coming out of our TV screens. If we did, people would pay money to watch me begin a simple plumbing repair at 8:00 a.m., make four trips to Home Depot for parts, flood the bathroom, and witness me proclaim the job complete at 4:30 p.m., convinced somehow that the remaining slow drip by the outlet valve would eventually go away by itself.

A lot of everyday talk about the real world perplexes me because it takes on contradictory meanings. At times, "real world" designates the grungiest and grittiest our environment has to offer. This real world is one where people use and betray each other, although it is never explained why the base and evil is more real than the beautiful and kind. However, reality TV puts a different spin on the idea of a real world. Through the magic of television, a situation in which a bachelor or bachelorette can hang out in a mansion and pick their future mate from a couple dozen of the most perfect physical specimens on earth (who use and betray each other) becomes "reality." I'm confused. If nothing else, this dichotomy should make us realize that reality doesn't mean the same thing for everyone.

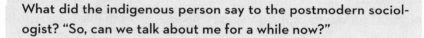

What did the indigenous person say to the postmodern sociologist? "So, can we talk about me for a while now?"

Our attempt to find a helpful Christian anthropology is not a secondary task. If our notions about human nature do not match the reality of how God has created us, this will skew our views of every other area of Christian doctrine. Whether we recognize it or not, humor weighs in on this debate. While other philosophies want to reduce us to only a soul or a body, humor grounds human nature in our hybrid existence. It reminds us that we are not just animal or angel but are odd existences who straddle both the animal and the divine worlds (Ps 8:5; Heb 2:7). In short, the only reason humor about us is humorous is because it talks about us as we know we really are. Humor can challenge reality, but it can't ignore it.

The significance of talking about ourselves for a while is so obvious that it frequently eludes us: if the Bible doesn't talk about real people as they really are, it has no relevance to us. I have placed my trust in Scripture because it tells me the truth about myself. It tells me I'm mortal but capable of grasping immortality. Scripture knows that I make moral judgments about what should be mourned or celebrated at the same time it knows that I get thirsty or sleepy. It knows that I am susceptible to both spiritual and physical illness. It tells me that being besieged by a coughing fit in the middle of leading the congregation in the Lord's Prayer is very human, and also a bit funny (after you've recovered from the embarrassment).

One payoff of seeing ourselves as God's humorous creation is that our laughter becomes a way of hugging human life, embracing it while acknowledging its oddities and ambiguities. Gnosticism and naturalism both recognize the incongruent worlds we occupy; the difference is that they just flat out don't like it. Thus, each attempts to overcome the incongruity either by denial (naturalism) or by proclaiming it tragic (gnosticism). Humor, in contrast, delights in the incongruous. It rolls around in it. Scripture also seems to revel in it because it tells us right up front that we are potting soil with a breath of divinity (Gen 2:7). This affirms both the finitude of our material being and the mysterious Godlike capacities of human nature as good, and allows us to enjoy the messiness that ensues from our unique existence. It also allows us to recognize that God does not desire to save us *from* our humanity, but to save us *in* our humanity.

> I think the Mr. Universe contest is rigged. Every year, it's been won by an earthling.

A second payoff of a humorous view of human nature is that the same tools that allow us to get the joke are those that allow us to get the message of God's grace. Humor notices that qualities that we usually think will exclude each other still, strangely, coexist. In humor, the expected outcomes of one set of truths are often replaced by a surprise ending. This also happens in Scripture. For example, within the created order, the sheer magnitude of God's work—"your heavens, the work of your fingers, the moon and the stars that you have established"—cues up a joke by raising an obvious question: "What are human beings that you are mindful of them, mortals that you care for them?" Then we hear God's gracious punch line that reverses what seems to be the logical answer. Instead of being confronted with the insignificance of our puny and short lives in an overwhelmingly huge cosmos, the unexpected is heard: "Yet you [God] have . . . crowned them [human beings] with glory and honor. You have given them dominion over the works of your hands; you have put all things under their feet" (Ps 8:3-6).

The psalmist makes it clear that, apart from God's gracious and humorous redefinition of human finitude, our situation is dire. Within the universe, our planet is an imperceptible speck, and we are an imperceptible speck on this planet. Why, indeed, should God care about us? Apart from grace, God would only laugh at our pretentions. With God's gracious "yet," however, we earthlings occupy a unique place in the universe. God's laughter is for us as he crowns us with glory and honor, even if we aren't all crowned Mr. Universe.

PUTTING ON A GOOD SHOW FOR GOD

 If God is watching us, the least we could do is make it entertaining.

I'm not sure what it might mean to entertain God, but I'm certain it's a more accurate description of God's response to us than the assumption that God is somehow disappointed with humanity. Many Christians act as if we should be embarrassed by embodiment, as if Adam and Eve escaped from God's lab and started breeding before the beta-testing phase was complete. In fact, it seems a tad ironic that those Christians who seem most disappointed in humans are also most likely to emphasize God's sovereignty and perfection. If God had intended to create beings who were more reflective of God's character and will, could he not have pulled that off? This seems more in line with what we know about God, to believe that God actually intended to create beings who write hymns *and* belch. Until we grasp the reality that God loves our entire embodied being, we won't fully recognize what brings God delight.

Scripture and our own experience reveal that we participate in two worlds simultaneously—the material and the soulish. Each dimension functions by different rules, but neither exists apart from the other. No matter how hard we may try to separate them, one world always pries its way into the picture, even if we don't want to recognize it. However, this combination of worlds often seems so incongruous and odd that history is full of anti-humorous philosophies and religions that downplay or dismiss either the meat and saliva parts of our being or the aesthetic and spiritual dimensions. Stated more directly, Christianity's view of the human as simultaneously spirit and dirt is constantly under challenge, sometimes from within, by views of human nature that are anti-humorous.

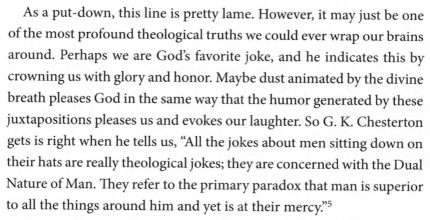

If you don't believe God has a sense of humor, just look in the mirror.

As a put-down, this line is pretty lame. However, it may just be one of the most profound theological truths we could ever wrap our brains around. Perhaps we are God's favorite joke, and he indicates this by crowning us with glory and honor. Maybe dust animated by the divine breath pleases God in the same way that the humor generated by these juxtapositions pleases us and evokes our laughter. So G. K. Chesterton gets is right when he tells us, "All the jokes about men sitting down on their hats are really theological jokes; they are concerned with the Dual Nature of Man. They refer to the primary paradox that man is superior to all the things around him and yet is at their mercy."[5]

Certain things aren't true, but they really should be. For example, the words *humor* and *human* sound so similar that we might think they come from the same root word. Unfortunately, it's unlikely that they do.

---

[5]G. K. Chesterton, "Cockneys and Their Jokes," in *All Things Considered* (New York: Sheed and Ward, 1956), 12.

Even though they lack a common etymological root, it seems almost impossible to think of real human beings without a chuckle. We are fundamentally funny creatures, and because human nature touches every dimension of our being, much more could be said about the profoundly beautiful, confounding, and funny character of our dichotomous nature. But I'll stop here. I'm hungry, and my butt itches.

3

HIGH HOLY DAYS,
PART ONE: CHRISTMAS

CHURCH CALENDARS

> I finally quit my job at the calendar factory. They would never let me take a day off.

> It's been a month since Chinese New Year, but I'm still writing "Year of the Rat" on all my checks.

Without calendars on my wall, computer, and cell phone, my life would be in total disarray. I would forget, even more than I now do, what I am supposed to be doing and when I am supposed to be doing it. Christians have understood the need for calendars for centuries, so we created a liturgical calendar to remind us of critical whats and whens so our spiritual life wouldn't become an incoherent mess. Of course, as with everything else in Christianity, the various segments of the church can't quite agree on the specifics of this calendar, or even if we should have such a thing. Despite these quibbles, Christians at least can concur on one thing: Christmas and Easter are the high points in the Christian year. If nothing else, it's good to know that we can agree that incarnation and resurrection are essential to our faith.

I come from a low-church tradition that doesn't do vestments color-coded to the seasons of the Christian calendar. If I talked about vestments at my church, most would assume I was referring to stocks, IRAs,

51

and 401(k)s. Most of my fellow congregants don't give up stuff like chocolate or watching college basketball for Lent and probably assume that "Shark Week" follows the celebration of Pentecost on the church calendar. However, all Christians seem to know that the time leading up to Easter is a season of self-examination and repentance. Along with our liturgical cousins, we less-cultured Christians join them in singing "O Come, O Come Emmanuel" in its minor key during Advent, remembering that we too are "captive Israel" awaiting "ransom" in confidence that Emmanuel will come. With our liturgical brethren, we ride the emotional roller coaster of Holy Week, which takes us from highs of the triumphal entry to the lows of the Messiah's betrayal, suffering, and death. The culminations of these preparatory periods are, of course, Christmas and Easter, times of joy when we remember the coming of God's Messiah and the Messiah's resurrection.

The point is that all Christians seem to have a clear picture about how we are supposed to worship God during those times when we remember how God disrupts the ordinary and mundane by taking on flesh, overturning death, and sending the Holy Spirit to invade the world. We "get" the high holy days. In chapter five, I will argue that we are not nearly as clear about how we should get almost two-thirds of the liturgical calendar, those large swaths of the years called Ordinary Time. However, in the next two chapters, I want to look at how humor may help see these high holy times in new ways and feel an even greater sense of how God is *for* us.

HILARIOUS HIGH HOLY DAYS

If we are attuned to Scripture's sense of humor, some things are laugh-out-loud funny. However, humor doesn't manifest itself in ways of side-splitting laughter in the Bible's reports of Christmas and Easter. Yet at almost every turn, we encounter those I-didn't-see-that-coming moments that are essential for humor. Women who can't get pregnant do,

Jewish religious experts looking for the Messiah cause Jesus to be crucified as a criminal while a dying criminal recognizes Jesus as the Messiah the Jewish leaders looked for, and women are the first witnesses of a risen Jesus while Jesus' closest disciples throw cold water on their reports. Thus, these stories are not "funny ha-ha" but "funny surprising." A lot of unexpected weirdness hides in plain sight, but the stories have become so familiar that we fail to see jaw-dropping surprises in the ways God rains his grace on us. In fact, because the Christmas and Easter narratives have so many comedic twists and turns, I will devote a chapter to each of the high holy times that are so crucial to our Christian story.

To get the full comedic impact of the first Christmas and Easter, we need to put ourselves in the shoes (or sandals) of the eyewitnesses. It is clear that they were thoroughly confused about it all. Everything about Christmas surprised the Jewish scholars who were looking for a messiah, and Jesus' disciples, who had spent years with him, had no Easter clue what was going on until some time after the resurrection. God authors one plot twist after another during these holy events and goes outside of casting stereotypes to find heroines and heroes. The surprise and reversal characteristic of the holy days says simultaneously that God will keep his promise to save his people, but that he is going to do it on his terms and in character with who he is.

INCARNATION JUXTAPOSITION CELEBRATION

> Oscar Madison to Felix Unger: "Look at this. You're the only man in the world with clenched hair."
>
> **THE ODD COUPLE**

If you agreed with the main premise of the previous chapter—that the combination of the material and the godlike in humans is funny—we should expect Christmas stories to be at least as funny. After all, the incarnation says that Jesus shares in humanity's juxtaposition of soul and body, and then doubles down by saying that this same human Jesus is fully God. With this, then, we add a completely new level of apparent incongruity when we confess that the true God comes to earth and takes on every bit of our funny and incongruous humanity.

God *con carne*, a God with meat, is what we are really talking about when we use the word *incarnation*. But the shock of God's self-"en-meatment" gets lost (literally) in translation in the English-language equivalent. However, we should see the very word as jolting because it forces us to consider a picture of God we never would have come up with on our own. We have become so familiar with embodiment in its sinful state that we could never conceive it as a medium for God. Thus, incarnation has a double twist. If we get it, we can never think of God in the same way, nor can we think of our body and our humanity in the same manner. Until we gain some grasp of the incarnation, we have a hard time realizing that God gives us all a do-over. We are not saved *from* ourselves. We are saved *within* our meaty existence by a Savior who takes on all that we are.

> Once I saw this guy on a bridge about to jump. I said, "Don't do it!"
>
> He said, "Nobody loves me."
>
> I said, "God loves you. Do you believe in God?"
>
> He said, "Yes."
>
> I said, "Are you a Christian or a Jew?"
>
> He said, "A Christian."
>
> I said, "Me, too! Protestant or Catholic?"
>
> He said, "Protestant."
>
> I said, "Me, too! What franchise?"
>
> He said, "Baptist."
>
> I said, "Me, too! Northern Baptist or Southern Baptist?"
>
> He said, "Northern Baptist."
>
> I said, "Me, too! Northern Conservative Baptist or Northern Liberal Baptist?"

> He said, "Northern Conservative Baptist."
>
> I said, "Me, too! Northern Conservative Baptist Great Lakes Region, or Northern Conservative Baptist Eastern Region?"
>
> He said, "Northern Conservative Baptist Great Lakes Region."
>
> I said, "Me, too! Northern Conservative Baptist Great Lakes Region Council of 1879, or Northern Conservative Baptist Great Lakes Region Council of 1912?"
>
> He said, "Northern Conservative Baptist Great Lakes Region Council of 1912."
>
> I said, "Die, heretic!" And I pushed him over.
>
> **EMO PHILIPS**

To remind ourselves of how odd it is to think of a god-human, we only need to look at two of the earliest and most persistent heresies within Christian history. The heresy on one end of the theological spectrum just can't buy the truly-God part of the Chalcedonian Creed. The most common early version of this is Arianism, which refused to accept the idea that a mere human could be united with the fullness of God. Thus, the Arians proclaimed that Jesus was not co-substantial with God but was instead similar to the Father. Jesus was "God-ish." This junior-varsity god still had sufficient divine resources to be our Savior and was created by the varsity god for this purpose. But the Arians couldn't find a way to believe that the God of gods would become human.

At the other end of the theological spectrum was Docetism—from the Greek word *dokéō,* meaning "to seem" or "appear"—which also believed that God can't take on real humanity. However, instead of demoting the divinity of Jesus, they denied his full humanity. Docetists argued that Jesus' body was fake meat, a mere phantom that left no footprints on the sand when he walked. This a real bummer for fans of the "Footprints in the Sand" poster,[1] where the single set of footprints

---

[1] If you are unfamiliar with this poem, here's a link: www.footprints-inthe-sand.com/index .php?page=Poem/Poem.php.

in the sand is supposed to belong to Jesus, who is carrying you in your struggles (*"And that big dent in the sand beside my footprints? That was accidentally where I dropped you. Sorry, but you were getting a bit heavy"*). Other versions of Docetism have argued that the divine Christ was like a ghost who entered the body of the human Jesus, allowed Jesus to do miraculous things during his ministry years, and then bailed out on the human Jesus before the suffering and crucifixion.

These heresies and their variants that go by fancy names like Monophysitism, Nestorianism, Psilanthropism, Adoptionism, Apollonarianism, and Northern Conservative Baptist Great Lakes Region Council of 1912 get something right.[2] They recognize the vast chasm that separates humanity and the divine, and the unity of the two just seems like an irresolvable contradiction. Thus, they are convinced that we have to fudge on one side or the other to make things fit comfortably. However, they wrongly interpret the apposition of the divine and the human as opposition and thus seek to remove it. Without juxtaposition, however, we lose the possibility of seeing incarnation as an example of God's good humor, and the heretics once again are exposed as anti-humorists.

While I'm not a fan of heresy (or humorlessness), I can't help but feel that maybe the christological heretics are in a better place theologically than many Christians who speak of the incarnation without any awareness of how mind-boggling the concept really is. The orthodox often blithely repeat the creeds without feeling the shock of what we confess, and this too is a form of humorlessness. However, there is a third option: we can grasp the full oddity of the incarnation with eyes wide open and still join orthodox Christians in confessing a real God who is joined to (and juxtaposed with) a very real human. One reason I encourage a humorous hermeneutic is precisely because it allows us to hold the fully human/fully divine tension in place. This

---

[2]If you want to get a sense of the importance the early church placed on getting Christology right, check out the Chalcedonian Creed (451 CE), which attempts to plug all of the holes that arose in these heresies.

is particularly important because Jesus comes knocking in a form we don't immediately recognize as God incarnate. Thus, we often call this incarnation juxtaposition a mystery, and we should. It is a mystery that should make us smile as we read the Christmas story because it reminds us of how surprising God is in his saving work.

By himself, Oscar Madison is simply a sad slob. Likewise, Felix Unger on his own is nothing more than an unbearable OCD poster boy. When they come together in *The Odd Couple*, the juxtaposition of their very different personalities creates comic magic. While it is not a direct parallel, Christians also believe that when God combines himself with real humanity, we experience a salvific magic. God does not remain apart from his people but unites with our humanity in a mysterious manner. Because of this union, God does not bring salvation from afar, but in the most intimate way possible. Thus, for those who believe that salvation occurs when our souls soar into the atmosphere, free of the material world, it must seem odd to them when they see the God they crave so much heading the opposite direction and ending up on earth with a real body. When Gregory of Nazianzus says, "What he [Jesus] has not assumed cannot be healed,"[3] he reminds us that when God assumes flesh, he does so to heal us. It's another one of God's jokes for us.

AN UNEXPECTED SAVIOR

A commuter passed a billboard along the freeway every day that had the message, "In trouble? Don't know what to do next? Call Jesus," with an 800-number at the bottom.

One day, the commuter's curiosity got the best of him, and he pulled over and called the number, and a voice at the other end of the line said, "Give me your location and we'll be there soon."

Fifteen minutes later, a Hispanic guy in a tow truck showed up.

[3]Gregory of Nazianzus, *Letters on the Apollinarian Controversy*, "Letter to Cledonius the Priest against Apollinarius," Letter CI, *New Advent*, www.newadvent.org/fathers/3103a.htm.

When you were a kid, Christmas was a time of expectation. You had very clear ideas about what you wanted to show up under the tree. If those expectations were dashed, deep disappointment followed. Parents know this, so I don't know what mine were thinking. I'm very sure my parents loved me, but when I was about nine years old, my parents did something unimaginable. One of the Christmas presents I received from them that year was soap on a rope. Soap, in any form, has zero allure to a nine-year-old boy. It is a commodity, not a gift. Putting soap on a strand of rope adds absolutely no value to it. Whose idea was this anyway?

The Jews of Jesus' day had high expectations about Christmas, although they didn't call it that. Moreover, their period of anticipation lasted much longer than the arrival of the Sears Christmas catalog, which used to be the official beginning of a kid's Advent season (yes, I'm that old), but this season for the Jews stretched back for centuries. They weren't completely united in what they were looking for in a savior, but they were sure he would be someone amazing: a warrior, a new king, an insightful teacher, or an uber-prophet. The Jesus who showed up was something quite different from their expectations. Not a tow-truck driver, but still different. Misidentification is one of the most common forms of comedy, and so it is humorous that their Messiah was hiding in plain sight. But the infant Jesus was not the Christmas present they were anticipating.

> Regardless of which family tree you shake, some nuts are bound to fall out.

Even before he gets to his version of the Christmas story, Matthew gives us a broad hint that God's Messiah is going to be a surprise. In line with Jewish expectations, Matthew gives a genealogy (Mt 1:1-17) that connects the coming Messiah with Jewish history by tracing three sets of fourteen (seven times two) generations: Abraham to David, David to exile, exile to Jesus. This list includes names that any good Jew would expect: Abraham, Jacob, David. But then things get weird. We also find names like Tamar, who tricks her father-in-law to get him to fulfill his duties (Gen 38:15). Rahab is a prostitute (Josh 2:1), but gains some level of redemption because she hides the spies scoping out the Promised Land. Ruth is the sorta good girl of the group but hardly fits the patriarchal or monarchical profile of a respectable genealogy. Bathsheba is the fourth female and was infamous for committing adultery with King David (not that she probably had much choice in this) and getting pregnant (2 Sam 11:1-13). Even odder is the fact that all four of these women are Gentiles—outsiders. The Jews were serious about their genealogies, and these four names would have screamed out that this was not, to put it mildly, the expected pedigree of God's anointed one. If Jesus' family tree includes Gentiles, prostitutes, adulterers, outsiders, and widows, it seems possible his future family may include those who are seen as beyond the reach of salvation.

PREGNANT VIRGINS AND OTHER SURPRISES

> Jesus had just arrived in heaven after his ascension, and the first person he saw was a white-haired man who looked vaguely familiar. Jesus asked him who he was and what he was doing at heaven's gates.
>
> The old man said, "I'm an old carpenter who is waiting for my son. He is not my son biologically. In fact, he came to be my son in the most unusual way. But I loved him as dearly as any father can love a son and cannot fully enjoy heaven until he arrives."
>
> Jesus, full of joy, shouts, "Father?"
>
> The old man looks back at him and says, "Pinocchio?"

Meanwhile over at Luke's Gospel, the pre-messianic events also take an unexpected turn. We might anticipate that a big God-thing would be transmitted through one of the temple priests, and that part syncs up with expectations. Zechariah, a priest, had been chosen by lot "to enter the sanctuary of the Lord and offer incense" (Lk 1:9). Entering the holy of holies may happen only once during his entire life, so this is the big time for a priest. Then, the unforeseen happens. An angel appears by the altar and announces that Zechariah's wife, who was beyond childbearing years, would become pregnant with a son. This son will be a new sort of Elijah, one who will "make ready a people prepared for the Lord" (Lk 1:17). This is great news in a double sense—the birth of the son Zechariah had long desired and the coming of the Messiah the Jews had awaited so many years. In fact, the news seems too good to be true, so Zechariah asks, "Are you kidding me?" The angel's response was, "Dude, I'm Gabriel. I don't kid about this sort of stuff" (Lk 1:18-19; note: the last two quotes are paraphrases of the Greek but are generally accurate in meaning). So Gabriel struck Zechariah speechless, literally, until the birth of his son, John, who is later known as John the Baptist. It's probably just as well. Who's going to believe what Zechariah has just learned?

A woman takes her sixteen-year-old daughter to the doctor. The doctor says, "Okay, Mrs. Jones, what's the problem?"

The mother says, "It's my daughter, Debbie. She's putting on weight and is sick most mornings."

The doctor gives Debbie a good examination, then turns to the mother and says, "Well, I don't know how to tell you this, but your Debbie is pregnant—about four months, would be my guess."

The mother says, "Pregnant?! She can't be. She has never ever been left alone with a man!"

Debbie says, "I've never even kissed a man!"

The doctor walks over to the window and just stares out. About five minutes pass and finally the mother says, "Is there something wrong out there, Doctor?"

The doctor replies, "Not really. It's just that the last time anything like this happened, a star appeared in the east and three wise men on camels came over the hill. I'm not going to miss it this time!"

60

Six months later, Gabriel shows up again. We rather expect angels to appear to priests, especially angels like Gabriel. However, this time he appears to a nobody, an unmarried but betrothed teenager named Mary. Gabriel is still in the baby-announcing business and tells Mary that she will become pregnant with a son who "will reign over the house of Jacob forever, and of his kingdom there will be no end" (Lk 1:33). News of one's pregnancy can be confusing, especially if you're a virgin, which Mary was. Gabriel assures her that the Holy Spirit will take care of the details and adds, "Oh, by the way, your elderly relative, Elizabeth (Zechariah's wife), is pregnant too."

When two women who should not be pregnant (though for different reasons) find themselves in such a state, it's probably safe to say that something unexpected is afoot. But Mary, perhaps because of her own low social status, seems to recognize that the baby she would soon deliver would be the deliverer of those who are like her. So she sings a song that includes these lyrics:

> He has shown strength with his arm;
> he has scattered the proud in the thoughts of their hearts.
> He has brought down the powerful from their thrones,
> and lifted up the lowly;
> he has filled the hungry with good things,
> and sent the rich away empty. (Lk 1:51-53)

Finally, we come to Joseph. He has an impressive pedigree as one who is in the line of David, but Joseph is also an "average Joe," plying his trade as a carpenter. He only plays a bit role in Scripture, but what little we know indicates that he wants to act honorably. When he finds out that his betrothed is pregnant, the obvious conclusion is that Mary has been unfaithful. He seeks to break the betrothal, but in a way that would not expose Mary (Mt 1:18-19). He too gets an angelic visitation, obviously one persuasive enough to convince him to continue their betrothal and eventually marry Mary.

Elizabeth, Zechariah, Mary, and Joseph are all in shameful situations —Elizabeth and Zechariah because of their childlessness, Mary and Joseph because of their unexplainable child*ful*ness. Shame is only possible in a social context, but God's new social reality has different rules. These four people have new identities that reverse the judgments of the old order. Reversal is one of humor's favorite tools, so we should laugh with Zechariah, Joseph, Elizabeth, and Mary when their shame is transformed into joy and blessing.

In the temporary empire that dominated this era, all four of these individuals remained nameless and obscure. In God's coming eternal kingdom, however, these nobodies and outcasts play central roles. In fact, the reversal of their status is so radical that we would not be surprised that Joseph, Elizabeth, and Zechariah were the greeting party for Jesus at his ascension. They live in a world in which God has rearranged all the furniture and creates a new reality. Still, we cannot forget that they are simultaneously embedded in the old social order, an order that kills the sons of both couples.

THAT COULDN'T HAPPEN HERE

As the pope was praying in his private chapel, his personal assistant entered. "Holy Father, I know it is highly unusual for me to interrupt your private prayers, but I have urgent news, both good and bad."

The pope said, "Well, my son, what is the good news?"

"Holy Father, Jesus has returned to earth, and he wants to talk with you on the phone."

The pope said, "This is wonderful news. What bad news do you bring?"

The assistant said, "He's calling from Salt Lake City."

As we try to imagine the first Christmas, our mind naturally goes to a stable with the holy family and their two sets of visitors. It's probably so familiar to us that we can almost repeat from memory the mashup of the Lukan and Matthean passages at the heart of the typical Christmas pageant. It's good to be familiar with such a vital part of our story, but it can feel so comfortable that we miss the oddness of it all, and important parts of the message as well.

When big things happen, we expect them to happen in big places. That's why media outlets are located in big places like Rome rather than Salt Lake City. Jewish expectations for a messiah who would be a new King David were strong, so we would think we would find him in Jerusalem, the center of David's kingdom. Yet, there may be hints even centuries before that messianic expectations of a new David were right, but folks would need to rethink which David would show up. Micah 5:2 refers us to David's hometown, Bethlehem, and notes that it is "one of the little clans of Judah." It doesn't even rise to Salt Lake City status. But perhaps Micah takes us behind David the mighty King of Jerusalem. Maybe he envisions instead David of Bethlehem, the obscure shepherd boy rather dismissively referred to by his father, Jesse, as "the youngest" (1 Sam 16:11).

Perhaps it a bit speculative to find parallels here with David the shepherd, but since shepherds play a big part in the story, the connection is certainly tempting. If you are looking for a hero who takes the side of the marginalized, the presence of shepherds might not be too shocking. They are certainly not among the power brokers. In fact, it is unlikely that they are frequent visitors to the temple because of their work. They exist on the edge of Judaism. So it is a bit surprising that these shepherds encounter the God who inhabits the holy of holies within the temple, a place where God received only one priestly guest per annum. But now even shepherds are invited to come and visit God. What an invitation it is. Singing angels and bright lights. It's hard to believe that the angel's instruction "Do not be afraid" (Lk 2:10) does much to calm the shepherds' anxiety. When something so overwhelming confronts them in the middle of nowhere on a dark night, fear seems appropriate. But when they go to see the baby, it impresses them enough that they tell everyone else about it. They seem to take it as a sign that God is opening branch offices in places like stables, the sort of places where shepherds feel at home.

The Magi make up another group of Christmas invitees with an interesting twist. On the one hand, we might not be surprised that God includes dignitaries as part of the Messiah's welcoming party. It also might not shock us to learn that the coming of the Savior would be accompanied by a star unusual enough to grab the attention of those who looked to the sky for signs of God's activity. On the other hand, many pieces in this story are totally unexpected. The story leaves open the possibility that the Magi were practitioners of a craft (astrology) condemned by Judaism. I'm almost certain they don't expect to discover that the baby they seek is in much less than luxury surroundings with poor, unmarried parents. In addition, these VIPs from the East throw the weirdest baby shower on record. Think about it. All guys, odd gifts, no games, and not a diaper in sight. To top it all off, they are Gentiles. The King of the Jews has Gentiles as guests for his arrival.

IT COULD BE A GREAT MOVIE

> Sad statistic: Twenty-five-thousand dyslexic children write Christmas letters to Satan each year.

> I have both ADHD and HDTV. I can't watch anything for too long, but the resolution is great.

Years back, a colleague forwarded a *TV Guide* description of a Christmas movie that read, "An angel comes to earth to restore a child's faith in Santa." If viewed through one set of eyes, it will strike some as a heart-warming story about hanging on to childlike innocence. To other eyes, however, it looks like sappiness on steroids, or at least one more reason to mourn the commercialization and secularization of the profound and holy. I'm reasonably certain that children losing faith in Santa is not our age's primary faith crisis.

If God were to produce a Christmas TV movie, the description might read something like this: "Angels come and completely freak out an old man with news that his equally old, barren wife was pregnant, a teenage virgin with news that she is pregnant, and a bunch of shepherds with 'glad tidings of great joy' that God has become a baby and he wants to see them ASAP." Studios would probably find the plot too far-fetched to ever greenlight such a movie (unlike zombie shows, of course) or claim that there just isn't enough of an audience for it. Actually, I think the audience for this story is huge because so many ache for a savior, especially one who seems so clearly on the side of those who are shut out of what our society generally views as salvific. I would watch it. I like salvation stories, even if they're a bit odd, or maybe *because* they are a bit odd. And I bet the angels and shepherds' music and light show would be awesome in high-def.

Despite the fact that I think a Nativity movie would be great TV, perhaps it is more on target to do what so many churches do: use the children of the congregation to tell the Christmas story. This never gets old for me. As the Nativity story comes to an end, the tableau is replete with fidgety shepherds in bathrobes wielding crooks that are likely to become weapons at any moment, the wise men look like escapees from a Mardi Gras party, and six-year-old angels (including some known to be anything but angelic) in white robes with frayed and bent tinsel halos. Mary and Joseph are always awkward because their peers will forever tag them as a "couple." I like this way of doing the story because these dynamics seem to be a close approximation of the first Christmas. None of the participants has much of a clue about the gravity of what is actually happening. But, as God so often does, he folds the least likely into his story and makes it theirs.

JOHN'S OFFENSIVE CHRISTMAS STORY

Toward the beginning of his "Seven Words You Can't Say on TV" routine, George Carlin notes, "There are words you can say, no problem. Topography! No one has ever gone to jail for screaming 'topography.' But there are some words that you can go to jail for."

Carlin continues by pointing out that some words are acceptable on TV in some contexts (such as using "bitch" to refer to a female animal) but are unacceptable in other cases (using the same term to refer to the next singer on the show). He labels such terms "two-way words."

On the other hand, he points out that some words are considered so offensive that they can't be uttered on TV at any time, and then goes on to say them with great gusto.

Carlin's 1972 "Seven Words" standup routine is still widely known today because it presses the ever-relevant ethical question: What do we consider offensive, and why? I plan to explore the relationship between humor and ethics in a future book, but for now we will be satisfied with two observations that Carlin highlights. First, words are powerful. Even an innocuous word like *topography* is capable of conveying an idea from one mind to another, an amazing feat that we overlook because it is so common. However, some words, often consisting of only four letters, carry such a wallop that they deeply violate one's moral, cultural, or theological convictions and cause us to wince internally. Second, using words deemed offensive within a humorous framework multiplies their power. Humor has always been a potent force when it comes to kicking the northern exposures of south-facing sacred cows, not least because it is performed before others and thus demands a response. So when Carlin proceeds to use a string of words generally considered offensive to challenge a taboo, the audience's laughter is a signal that, to some extent, they accept these offenses as permissible.

This rather longish introduction brings us to the Christmas story in John's Gospel (Jn 1:1-18). John's incarnation story is often overlooked during the Christmas season because it doesn't have the riveting action and colorful characters we find in the Lukan and Matthean accounts. However, like the two more popular Christmas stories, John's prologue offers plenty of comedic material. We have to look harder to see it because it is a heady, even philosophical, form of humor. Despite its more intellectual structure, John's prologue is not just humor but is intentionally offensive, even profane, humor.

There is a consensus that John addresses his Gospel to Jewish Christians living outside of Palestine. Thus, these believers participated in three worlds. By religious background they are Jewish, but because of the dispersion (Diaspora) of Jews to different corners of the empire, their Judaism had been marinated in Greek language and thought forms. These two factors remain in play when John's audience comes to Christianity through conversion, and we see it in the Jewish-Greek-Christian way John frames his Christmas story.

The opening phrase of the Gospel, "In the beginning" (Jn 1:1), would have perked up Jewish ears, signaling that what followed would parallel the Genesis story of creation, an intuition quickly confirmed by the phrase "all things came into being through him" (the *Logos*) two verses later. The humorous setup for John's offensive joke, however, comes from a single word that would have been flagged by the Greek side of their brains: "In the beginning was the Word" (Jn 1:1). In the Greek philosophical tradition, *Logos,* which we translate as "Word," is jam-packed with meaning.

When Greek philosophers wanted to talk about a perfect, unchanging, divine, and rational power that gives structure, order, and goodness to the universe, Logos was the go-to "God-Word." Thus, Logos does not simply refer to a verbal utterance, a word to which we assign a definition. Logos should make us think of a human logic (yes, you should see a relationship between these two words) that seeks the truth and purpose imposed on the universe by a divine logic/Logos. Logos, on the macro level, refers to the divine rationality that governs all creation as well as the rational power within each individual that expresses itself in linguistic ways. Our use of language and the rationality that makes this possible is, in a sense, our connection with the divine Logos. It's the *imago Dei* for Greek-thinking Christians.

When John's Gospel begins with, "In the beginning was the Word," John immediately builds a two-lane cultural bridge to his audience by using obvious cues from both their Jewish and Greek backgrounds. Except for some quibbles about details, most Diaspora Jews would have few reservations about any of this. However, John soon lets his audience know they have been set up. Not much later he throws in a punch line that he knows will make non-Christian Greek heads explode: "And the [Logos] became flesh" (Jn 1:14). For traditional Greek thinkers, this goes beyond illogic; a "flesh-becoming" Logos is offensive. The Greek Logos remains in its own world, strictly separated from materiality. Therefore, to claim that the Logos *becomes* flesh profanes that which is holy. John crosses a line by claiming that God violates the inviolable boundary that separates the divine and the fleshly by taking on meat.

For Greek thought, Logos was *Being*—pure, perfect, unchanging, and unchangeable. In contrast, flesh and other forms of materiality were *becoming*—transitory, imperfect, and partial. To combine Being with becoming was unconscionable and offensive. The pure doesn't cavort with the mortal and changeable. John, ignoring every standard of Greek decorum, combines Being and becoming in a dramatic way. While English translations of verse fourteen have the decency to separate Logos and flesh with a verb ("the Word *became* flesh"), John rubs our face in this juxtaposition. His Greek version crams Word right up next to flesh (materiality) and says, "Logos flesh became," or as Greeks would read it, "Being becoming became."

Our cultural context is different from that of John's first readers. Thus, when we read "the [Logos] became flesh," Christians say, "Yes. Of course." However, the original audience knew that Logos was, as Carlin put it, a "two-way" word. For the Greek, *Logos* is a culturally and religiously acceptable way to speak of the divine power that provides the material world's logical and predictable flow. It becomes reprehensible, however, when Logos gets tangled up in flesh and blood in a crucifiable human named Jesus.

I DON'T SEE YOUR LOGIC

> "God would never let me be successful. He'd kill me first. He'll never let me be happy."
>
> "I thought you didn't believe in God?"
>
> "I do for the bad things."
>
> **GEORGE COSTANZA TALKING WITH HIS THERAPIST,** *SEINFELD*

"I'm afraid I don't see your logic" is one of the nicest ways in the English language to say, "I've never heard anything so stupid in my entire life." George Costanza's line is funny precisely because it is illogical. God's existence is not contingent on how well or poorly things are going in your life. Based on its long-standing ideas about the Logos, "the world" couldn't see God's logic, and thus it "knew him not" (Jn 1:10 KJV). To Greek ears, identifying Jesus as Logos is more than stupid or provocative; it is offensive to community standards of decency and should be banned from the public airwaves. But, as it is with so many naughty jokes, while some in the audience are offended and may even howl about heresy, others will laugh in affirmation. John's Greek-Jewish Christians could only be Christians if they laughed along with God's incarnation joke. They knew that the Christian definition of Logos was taboo to the Greek mind, but they also came to believe that "Being becoming became" was true and transforming, and thus confessed, sometimes at mortal risk, that "God Jesus became." These early Christians came to believe that God's logic didn't always square with what the world considers logical, and they were considered profane and irreverent for it.

PEEKABOO

> I think peekaboo is easily the cruelest joke we play with children. This is because babies lack what we call "object permanence." So when you close their eyes, they don't know you still exist as their mother.
>
> The game should really be called "orphan, not orphan."
>
> **REID FAYLOR**

There is no sound purer and more beautiful than an infant's laughter, and I still find it amazing that we humans learn to laugh at such an early age. However, babies don't laugh at sitcoms or elephant jokes. I've tried it. Instead, the earliest trigger for human laughter is surprise; if you startle an infant, she will either laugh or cry. We evoke laughter in a young child by throwing her in the air and catching her, making an unexpected silly sound, or the perennial favorite, playing peekaboo. In a game of peekaboo, the baby is perplexed about where I've gone when I pull the blanket over my face. When I pull away the blanket and say, "Look, here I am!" she giggles and squirms.

The Christmas God turns the tables on our game of peekaboo because it is about an infant who pulls away the veil and says, "Look here, I AM!" It is appropriate to squirm, because we are just not used to thinking about God in this way. But the I AM of the burning bush, the *mysterium tremendum*, the God who causes us to quake and tremble, is also the I AM of the *mysterium fascinans*, the God who draws and attracts. This baby-God means that we are no longer orphans but have been incorporated into God's family. So giggling also seems appropriate. The infant Jesus-God takes on flesh, our flesh, and surprises us by redeeming it.

HIGH HOLY DAYS, PART TWO: EASTER

My wife and I decided we didn't want to have children. Our three kids aren't taking it well.

"Wow, honey. I never thought our son would go so far."
"Me either. This catapult is amazing. Go get our daughter."

This is dark humor. In comedic terms, both of these quips represent a skillful use of misdirection. That makes them funny, at least for some people. However, since both refer to mistreatment of children, others will say that it is inappropriate to laugh at such jokes, even if no one actually did these things. For many, the same will be true of looking at the events surrounding Easter through the filter of humor. Laughter seems out of place during Lent's time of repentance and Holy Week's remembrance of the suffering and death of Jesus. Gloom shrouds so much of this period, and it seems right that our attitudes reflect this.

Still, there is Easter. While we remain in the moment of Jesus' pain and suffering during much of Holy Week, Easter is the only reason we commemorate the events that lead to the cross. If suffering, injustice, and death are the sole point of it all, we should close down shop on Friday and double up on our antidepressant prescriptions. But if we celebrate *Good* Friday, we can do so only because we know that death doesn't get the final word. Friday's goodness is only possible because

Easter resurrection is on the horizon. Without the Easter reversal of death, we have no reason for Lent and Holy Week. Apart from the forgiveness that comes via the cross, the earlier season of repentance is a waste of time. If God does not vindicate the new kingdom that stands at the center of Jesus' message, we are stuck forever with nothing but Roman power politics in all the ugly variations it has assumed throughout history.

If there is nothing holy about Holy Week apart from Easter, what is the proper response when that day finally comes? In the medieval church, priests were encouraged to tell racy jokes during Easter mass to evoke laughter. This ritual was known as the *Risus Paschalis,* the Easter Laugh. In other words, it was considered inappropriate *not* to laugh on this most holy day, and priests would go to great lengths to make sure the church was filled with laughter in celebration of Christ's victory over death.[1]

Perhaps I'm too prudish, but I'm okay with skipping lewd jokes at the Easter service. However, I think our medieval sisters and brothers are dead right about the laughter part. After all, we don't just laugh when something is funny. We laugh from surprise. We laugh when astoundingly good things happen. Laughter is the release of tension that occurs when the worst seems inevitable and instead everything turns out better than we could have dreamed. Does the resurrection of Jesus seem to square up with these reasons for laughter?

If it is right to say that there can be no Christian observance of Lent or Holy Week apart from Easter, the Easter perspective means that we are in on the joke and are prepared already for God's punch lines. We have read ahead, so we know that God *redefines* the cross. It is no longer a source of social shame but is instead a symbol of glory. We have already seen the *irony* that Pilate's inscription that mockingly identifies

---

[1]Jürgen Moltmann, speaking of the *Risus Paschalis,* says, "The laughter of the universe is God's delight. It is the universal Easter laughter." Jürgen Moltmann, *The Coming of God: Christian Eschatology,* trans. Margaret Kohl (Philadelphia: Fortress Press, 2004), 339.

Jesus as King of the Jews is, after all, correct. If anything, Pilate understates the truth since Jesus is also king of the universe. The Jewish leaders throw Jesus to the Roman authorities because of their fear of insurrection, but they totally *misidentify* the sort of insurrection that Jesus came to foment. Most importantly, because we are reading the story backwards, we know that the death that was supposed to bring a decisive end to the life and work of Christ is *reversed* and instead ushers in eternal life for him and his followers. Redefinition, irony, misidentification, and reversal are all mainstays for the humorist, and they stand front and center in the saga that culminates in Easter.

The backdrop for the humor of the Easter events, once again, is incongruity. Instead of the body/soul incongruity of chapter two, or the divine/human juxtaposition of chapter three, here we have a sense of disparity in which the future celebration of God's vindication of Jesus bleeds back into our mourning and horror at the injustice of Jesus' suffering. We feel anguish, confusion, and loss as Jesus commends his spirit into God's hands (Lk 23:46), but this exists alongside our confidence and joy that death is overturned. The ugliness of our sin and the beauty of God's forgiveness stand together as we experience the Easter cycle. As in so many humorous scenarios, these look like oppositions that simply cannot occupy the same space and time, but Easter demands that we maintain the tension.

While gallows humor is often present in the darkest moments of our life, we also find "cross humor" in the darkest moments of our faith. Lent reminds us of this, because its forty days of fasting and repentance are interrupted six times when Sunday rolls around. On the church's calendar, every Sunday is a memorial to the resurrection, a feast day. So even in the Lenten period of repentance and self-denial, we open the drapes once a week, remind ourselves that the sun is still shining, and eat a Snickers bar before we return to our chocolate fast on Monday.

Easter's humor has a shadow side, but darkness is eventually overcome. So Easter's dark humor stands in contrast to the two jokes at the top of the chapter. Even though every parent has probably envisioned similar actions at some point in the child-rearing process, hurtling your kid across the neighborhood with a catapult is not a redemptive activity, and fetching a sibling to reload it simply doubles down on the darkness. If a couple decides not to have children, that's okay with most of us. It's not okay when people make that choice after producing three offspring. It's dark, but the Easter story doesn't end in darkness. Instead, it redeems it. As Rodney Clapp puts it: "In the crucifixion of Jesus Christ, the worst that the world can do has been done. And with the world's worst, God wrought the world's best. God brings not only the world's survival, but its flourishing, out of the darkest of all human acts."[2] The darkness was and is real, but it is not ultimate. Life and light prevail.

PASSOVER/NEW EXODUS

Foot: A device well adapted for geo-locating LEGOS in the dark.

Sweater: A garment worn by children when their mother gets cold.

URBAN DICTIONARY

Instead of remaining in the realm of the abstract, let's look at a concrete example of how we already read the joyfulness of the future back into the bleakness of the Passion narratives. The Gospels tell us that the chief priests and scribes begin their scheme to kill Jesus on the cusp of Passover (Mk 14:1), the holiest day of the year for their people. It is ironic and grimly humorous that those with primary responsibility for the spiritual well-being of their people

---

[2]Rodney Clapp, *New Creation: A Primer on Living in the Time Between the Times* (Eugene, OR: Cascade, 2018), 121.

are preoccupied with eliminating one of their own instead of focusing on how this most holy commemoration will bless the Jewish nation. Moreover, the one they want to kill is the very Messiah they so ardently seek. It can be funny when someone misses the point completely, but this has awful consequences.

When Passover comes, Jesus and his disciples celebrate it together. At least it is supposed to be a celebration. However, Jesus dumps a bucket of ice water on the festivities by telling the group that one who is at the table and who has been with him during his earthly ministry will betray him. Jesus raises the ante with a second prediction: another close to him will deny him before the night is over. It is right that we mourn where these two betrayals will lead, but it also seems right that a slight smile crosses our face as we anticipate something else. Just prior to dropping the bomb about his coming betrayal, Jesus engaged in an act of redefinition. He "took a loaf of bread, and when he had given thanks, he broke it and gave it to them, saying, 'This is my body, which is given for you. Do this in remembrance of me.' And he did the same with the cup after supper, saying, 'This cup that is poured out for you is the new covenant in my blood'" (Lk 22:19-20; compare Mk 14:22-24).

Bread and wine were mainstays of the Passover, but only in retrospect could his disciples comprehend the double redefinition of these grocery items. Soon they would learn that the broken body and spilled blood refer to Jesus' death. However, resurrection adds a new and paradoxical re-redefinition to bread and wine because new life and forgiveness are found through them. The bloodied, broken body is also the resurrected body. As a result, when the disciples participate in the covenant meal of bread and wine after Jesus' resurrection, it's the celebration that the Last Supper could not be. Just as humor redefines terms so that they take on new meaning, Jesus' redefinition of bread and wine means that they do not cease to be what they are, but they can no longer be only what they are.

LIFE FROM DEATH

 If vegetarians only eat vegetables, what do humanitarians eat?

One of the ironies of life is that we have to eat dead stuff to stay alive. Vegetarians recognize this, thus their objections to the raising and slaughter of animals to satisfy our appetites. And the poor chicken. It's eaten both before it's born and after it's dead. The carnivore's response is, of course, that animals shouldn't be made of meat if we are not supposed to eat them. In addition, they argue, the vegetarian is also guilty of slaughter. We sacrifice the innocent lives of plants, fruits, and grains to prepare that tofu surprise, and each bowl of quinoa contains a thousand tiny, edible, organic corpses.

My silly detour into our contemporary food fights shouldn't mask two truths. Our physical life relies on death, and our spiritual nourishment requires Jesus' death. The latter entails the juxtaposition of our sorrow and our joy. When Paul repeats Jesus' words that institute the Lord's Supper, he reminds us that these were spoken "on the night when he [Jesus] was betrayed" (1 Cor 11:23). Thus, we should feel a double twinge. Not only is Judas's betrayal a crucial step leading to Jesus' death, but we are complicit in it. At the same time, we *celebrate* the Lord's Supper. In fact, some Christian traditions refer to it as Eucharist—thanksgiving (*not to be confused with "euchre wrist," a malady afflicting Christians who play card games too often*).

When we read about the night Jesus was betrayed, bitter tears and giddy laughter collide with each other. This combination doesn't seem fully compatible, but we also know that both are appropriate as signals that we clearly understand what happened and what is happening. The Passover meal Jesus ate with his disciples to remember Israel's liberation from slavery is redefined as the new Israel's liberation from the slavery of sin. Nevertheless, the route of this new exodus runs through the cross.

THEY SHOULD KNOW BETTER

> I was sitting on a plane that is traveling towards Seattle. And the guy next to me turns and says to me, "Hey, you going to Seattle?"
>
> "Nope, San Francisco . . . I'll be parachuting off in about an hour." Here's your sign!
>
> I pull up at the Christmas-tree shop and I walk up and the guy says "Hey, you here to buy a tree?"
>
> "Nope, my son had to go to the bathroom and these trees looked mighty inviting." Here's your sign!
>
> **BILL ENGVALL**

Bill Engvall frequently includes a "Here's your sign" segment in his standup routine that requires no explanation to his fans. For the uninitiated, however, this phrase builds on the observation that people often say mind-bogglingly stupid things about what should be obvious to anyone. The premise is that those prone to make such statements should be required to wear an "I'm stupid" sign to warn everyone else of their condition.

The Bible is full of here's-your-sign examples where people just don't get what seems to be obvious. At the risk of sounding disrespectful to men who now have the word *Saint* as a title to their names, the level of misunderstanding and sheer stupidity of Jesus' closest followers from the Last Supper to the crucifixion is darkly comical. This is, after all, Jesus' inner circle. They have been with him an extended period, they have heard his teaching, and they have witnessed his miracles. Jesus told them what was going to happen to him. They really should have this figured out, but they clearly don't.

We have already mentioned that Jesus' betrayal is an inside job (Lk 22:48). We also know that Peter swears to Jesus that he is willing to go with Jesus "to prison and to death" (Lk 22:33) and then throws him under the bus not once but three times just a few hours later (Lk 22:54-62). Add to this the fact that the disciples choose "which one of them was to be regarded as the greatest" as the post-Passover dinner topic (Lk 22:24). After what Jesus has just revealed about betrayal and denial at their Passover meal, does this seem appropriate?

Apparently, the bar for the greatest disciple was pretty low because when Jesus goes to pray at Gethsemane after the Last Supper, the disciples' only job is to stay awake and pray with him. Yet within moments they are all sleeping off their Passover meal. In fact, Mark's account has Jesus returning to awaken them three different times (Mk 14:37-41). To top it off, when Judas arrives with the chief priests, Pharisees, and soldiers to betray Jesus, one of the disciples (John's Gospel fingers Peter; other accounts leave out the name) lops off the ear of the chief priest's servant. In addition to all of Peter's other missteps that evening, he is also singled out for rebuke by Jesus for dozing off during Gethsemane prayer time (Mk 14:37). Scripture is silent about who won the which-disciple-is-the-greatest contest earlier that evening, but it's unlikely that Peter got Jesus' vote.

The disciples' performances on Passover night are disappointing to say the least, and it doesn't get much better for a while. When Jesus appears to them on Easter evening, they are behind locked doors "for fear of the Jews" (Jn 20:19). In fact, only twice are any of the disciples mentioned between Peter's betrayal and the Easter-evening appearance—a rather cryptic reference to the disciple "whom he [Jesus] loved" (Jn 19:26) at the foot of the cross, and the Easter-morning race to the tomb (5K?) between Peter and "the other disciple" (Jn 20:2, 3, 4, 8). Otherwise, collectively they are completely AWOL. We get references to women at the cross, preparing Jesus' body for burial, and being the first visitors to show up at the tomb on Sunday morning. Simon of Cyrene, Nicodemus, and Joseph of Arimathea all make an appearance in the intervening period. The remaining disciples?

Almost totally absent. Their actions, or inactions, are enough to make you want to smack your forehead with the palm of your hand, provided you aren't wearing a crown of thorns. They really should have known better.

"You can't fix stupid" is a signature line for Ron White, a comedian who occasionally performs alongside Bill Engvall. Fortunately, White is wrong about stupidity as a terminal condition. The disciples' earlier cluelessness and fear is radically transformed into theological insight and admirable courage after the resurrection. Previously in the story, we found them cowering behind locked doors out of fear for their lives. Fifty days later at Pentecost, Peter, with the other disciples standing beside him in plain sight to all, gives a very public sermon (Acts 2:14-38). They're in the same city in which Jesus had been crucified. The same political and religious leaders are still in power. It was a feast time again, and the power brokers still had the same fears about unrest among the populace during such periods. All the factors that led to the crucifixion of Jesus are still in play, but the danger factor is now heightened. Peter is preaching that Jesus rose from the dead and the kingdom of God is here—not the sort of message the Jewish and Roman leaders want on the street after they thought they had taken care of all the Jesus stuff weeks earlier.

The actions of Peter and the other disciples are an abrupt contrast to what we saw prior to the resurrection, and this is only the beginning of very different lives for them. The historical record is foggy and incomplete, but we have good reasons to believe that the majority if not all worked diligently and courageously to spread the message of Jesus and eventually died as martyrs for the kingdom. The contrast between the before and after pictures of the disciples is stunning. While the pre-Easter failures and confusion of the Twelve are profound and real, we see the humorous and redemptive reversal that follows Easter. It was as if they too had been raised from the dead.

TANGLED POLITICAL WEBS

There was a massive traffic jam on the streets of Washington, DC. Before she could turn on the radio to hear what was happening, a man tapped on her car window.

"Terrorists have taken over Congress and are demanding a $100,000,000 ransom, or they'll douse them all with gasoline and set them on fire. We're collecting donations."

The woman asked, "So what's the average contribution?"

The man answered, "About a gallon."

As long as there are political figures, there will be political humor. They wield a great deal of power over our lives, and at times it seems that humor is our only defense against their often stupid and oppressive choices. A darkly humorous element of the Passion narratives is present in the political entanglements of the major players. The chief priests and scribes are the go-along-to-get-along toadies of the Roman government. They have a good gig going. The Romans gave them power and a degree of autonomy within their little Jewish pond, and they don't want the rabble to ruin things by getting carried away over some wannabe messiah (Lk 22:1-2). The Jewish rabble chafes at the yoke of the Romans and is looking for a messiah who will put a military hurt on their occupiers. However, the contrast between the triumphal entry (Mt 21:1-17; Mk 11:1-11; Lk 19:29-40; Jn 12:12-19) on Sunday when they greeted their candidate for King of Israel with "Hosanna!" and then their shouts of "Crucify him!" only a few days later indicates they are a fickle and unreliable lot. Pilate, the face of the Roman Empire in the region, knows that keeping his job, and maybe even his head, depends on keeping peace. When large numbers of Jews are in town to celebrate their most important feast, religious fervor is strong, rumors travel quickly, and things can be volatile. Then we have hapless Herod, a

Jewish king with limited powers caught between the Jewish religious power brokers, the masses, and the Roman government.

The complications created by these tangled political webs are on full display in the various trials of Jesus. After Jesus' arrest, the chief priests' case against him is not going well in the early stages. Their witnesses keep contradicting each other (Mk 14:56, 59), and it looks like Jesus may get to walk. However, the trial quickly takes a turn. When the high priest asks Jesus if he is the Messiah, he gives the fateful "I am" answer (Mk 14:62). They have what they view as a blasphemous statement, but one small problem remains. The Jewish leaders don't have authority to sentence someone to death, so Jesus lands on Pilate's doorstep.

When Pilate asks Jesus if he is "King of the Jews," he doesn't receive an unambiguous answer (Mt 27:11) and concludes that he can find no reason to execute Jesus. Pilate clearly doesn't want to handle this hot potato and passes him off to Herod. At first, Herod is anxious to meet Jesus, but only because he wants Jesus to do some magic (Lk 23:8). When Jesus won't perform for him and doesn't even respond to his inquiries, Herod's mood sours quickly. Herod is a king, and Jesus has no Miranda rights to remain silent before a king. In a snit, he mockingly puts a royal robe on him and bounces him back to Pilate.

It seems clear that Pilate, who once again states that he finds no evidence of guilt, has no stomach for crucifying Jesus and tries to take a middle route by having him beaten (Lk 23:16). Finally, confronted by the insistence of the crowd that Jesus be put to death, Pilate does a swap, giving them Barabbas, an insurrectionist and murderer, in exchange for Jesus (Lk 23:24-25). Jesus has been whipped to the point of death, but it is Pilate who is totally at a loss about what to do with Jesus. The serene yet forceful Jesus stands before the person who holds his life in the balance, and it is Pilate who is in a state of panic. In a feeble attempt to absolve himself of blame, he washes his hands (Mt 27:24).

The funny thing about these events is that those considered politically powerful are motivated by fear at every turn. What sort of power is that? There is something comedic in the fact that the Romans rightly see Jesus as a challenge to all they stand for but at the same time totally miss the point of his kingdom. Thus, the one whose kingdom is not of this world is executed by those who are attempting to preserve their puny slice of a worldly kingdom. The humorous twist in this is that Barabbas, the insurrectionist set free in exchange for Jesus, desires to start the sort of rebellion feared by the Jewish and Roman leaders, while Jesus has no interest in this sort of power. When Pilate reminds Jesus that he has the authority to have Jesus crucified, Jesus' response is that any power Pilate has comes from God (Jn 19:11). For someone invested in the idea that Rome is the ultimate source of all power, I'm sure Jesus' answer baffled Pilate. For those who believe that we must all justify ourselves to Rome, Jesus' silence made no sense.

Despite their inability to make sense of what Jesus is about, both Herod and Pilate do get some things right. For example, both pronounce him innocent of any wrongdoing. In fact, Pilate does so twice. Of course, then Pilate has the innocent Jesus executed anyway. In addition, few things are quite as ironic as the fact that Pilate gets it right when the placard on the cross proclaims Jesus of Nazareth as "King of the Jews." The chief priests are not at all happy about the inscription, but Pilate insists that it remain on the cross. He doesn't get what Jesus' kingdom is about at all; his intention is to ridicule. Yet he tells the truth about Jesus' kingship—in three languages, no less (Jn 19:19-22). Herod derisively clothes Jesus in a royal robe, and the attire is ironically appropriate. Finally, Pilate's soldiers crown Jesus with thorns and mock him as the King of the Jews (Jn 19:3). In hindsight, it's funny because it turns out they were right. It almost makes you wonder whether there is a certain playfulness about God. Even if they fail to understand who Jesus really is, God sees to it that these political power-players somehow can't help but speak the truth about his identity.

REDEFINING CRUCIFIXION

 Death: The exact moment at which a person stops sinning.

It's hard to think of a more gruesome form of execution than crucifixion. That was the intent. The slow and painful process was a public exhibition of what and who the Romans considered contemptible. Crucifixion was not allowed as a mode of execution for Roman citizens, no matter how despicable their offenses. Instead, it was a reminder to all occupied people that Rome was in charge. Crucifixion was a mark of shame, the ultimate symbol of powerlessness and insignificance. For those who saw Jesus as a king, the cross was intended to be a decisive and bloody counterargument: Your king is powerless against the empire.

Apparently, my church has an ironic sense of humor. During Lent, a ten-foot-tall cross is placed front and center in our sanctuary. Around the base of the cross are the accompanying tools of torture, shame, and mockery: a whip, large nails, and a crown of thorns. Instead of being ashamed of our association with the cross, however, our church views it as a sign of victory and glory. There's precedent for this. Not even two months after Jesus was crucified, Peter built his Pentecost sermon around the cross. Even though everyone who heard him was intimately familiar with the shame of crucifixion, Peter doesn't hide it. He revels in it. Peter tells the Pentecost crowd that Jesus is the crucified one, *but* God made him "Lord and Messiah" (Acts 2:36). Jesus is the crucified one, *but* "God raised him up" (Acts 2:24). If I'm reading this right, Peter seems to be saying that Rome's evaluation of Jesus as shameful has been reversed by a higher power. The *but* makes all the difference. Rome played its strongest card, and God trumps it (for those of you who don't play cards, it's just a figure of speech). While Jesus was raised up on a cross in shame, God raised him up from the tomb and exalted him as Lord. Thus, the church birthed on that Pentecost day would be defined by the cross, but this was possible only because the cross was redefined by God.

Because the Roman Empire consisted of a vast patchwork of cultures and religions, there was no uniformity of belief about what happens to a person postmortem. Even though the notion of resurrection was present in the Judaism of Jesus' day, it was not a unanimous position. The Sadducees did not believe in life after death at all (that's why they're sad-you-see) because the Torah didn't provide evidence of such a doctrine, while some Diaspora Jews embraced immortality of the soul rather than resurrection.[3] But one thing both Roman and Jewish leaders assumed was that crucifixion would put an end to Jesus and whatever mission he and his motley band of followers were up to. After all, this was not their first encounter with messianic movements. Experience had taught them that if you cut off the head, the whole beast dies. Killing Jesus in the ghastliest way possible would be enough to send his disciples packing.

The events of that Friday seem to confirm all the assumptions of the crucifiers. The disciples are nowhere to be seen, the women weep in despair, and the blood and water flow from Jesus' side. Jesus' words "It is finished" (Jn 19:30) give the air of finality to the whole story. Little does anyone know that this is the setup. The punch line comes on the third day, with the ultimate reversal and redefinition of death. The death sentence imposed by Pilate is overturned on appeal to God, and the cross that was a symbol of shame now becomes the means by which the shame of our sin is wiped out. Thus, while our death is the point at which we stop sinning, Jesus' death is the moment at which God stops sin.

It is hard to get more ironic than the cross. The silent one who doesn't defend himself against those holding the reins of political power defeats an empire by sacrifice and death. The only truly pure person is crucified as a criminal, and then an actual criminal enters Paradise (Lk 23:43) well ahead of those obsessed with religious purity. An empire

---

[3]For an overview of Jewish concepts of postmortem existence, see Simcha Paul Raphael, *Jewish Views of the Afterlife*, 2nd ed. (Lanham, MD: Rowman & Littlefield, 2009).

bristling with weapons of mass destruction is helpless to stop a kingdom whose only weapons are goodness and light. Death, which is supposed to be final, turns out to be part of a bigger process that leads once again to life. We are tempted to call it ironic because it is odd. There is something strange and seemingly contradictory about it all, and this is where humor arises. But there is more to it than just oddness. Viewed from the Christian perspective, irony is revelatory because it tells us new and deeper truths about God and God's kingdom.

SEEING, AND NOT SEEING, A RESURRECTED JESUS

A magician worked for a cruise line. Since he would get a completely new audience every few days, he repeated the same magic tricks. The ship captain's pet parrot came to every show and eventually figured out the magician's illusions. Soon, the parrot spoiled every trick by saying, "All the cards in the deck are the ace of spades"; "The ball is up his sleeve"; or "That's not the same hat."

One night, the parrot was once again about to reveal a trick's secret to the audience, and the magician had reached his limit. He grabbed a hatchet and threw it at the bird. Unfortunately, it missed the parrot and hit a propane tank, which exploded and blew up the entire ship.

Later, the magician was clinging to a piece of wood from the ship's wreckage, drifting in the ocean, and the parrot was sitting on the opposite end of the wood. For three days, they bobbed up and down in the water, just staring at each other. Finally, the parrot said, "Okay, I give up. What did you do with the ship?"

Who ya gonna believe? Me, or your own eyes?

CHICO MARX, *DUCK SOUP*

Unless I'm attending a magic show, I tend to think that what I see with my own eyes is a pretty good barometer of truth. If I must choose between whether I'm going to believe the claims of another person or what I have witnessed with my own eyes, the eyes have it, especially if the other person is as dodgy as one of the Marx brothers. However, when it comes to the post-resurrection appearances of Jesus, it seems that normal vision isn't too reliable. The two Emmaus travelers don't recognize him for hours (Lk 24:13-35). It's unclear how closely associated with Jesus they are, so we might be able to chalk this up to a lack of familiarity. However, there must be some degree of acquaintance with Jesus since they do eventually recognize him. And Mary Magdalene mistakes him for the gardener at the tomb (Jn 20:15-18).

Did the resurrected Jesus look that much different, or did they all fail to recognize him because no one expected to see him after his death? I suspect the latter has something to do with it. After all, when the women report the news of the empty tomb to the disciples, they dismiss it as "an idle tale" (Lk 24:11). The two Emmaus disciples are headed back home, which seems to indicate they see no reason to hang around Jerusalem and wait for Jesus to reappear. Even after Jesus appears to the disciples, Luke says, "While in their joy they were disbelieving and still wondering" (Lk 24:41). Thomas is so skeptical that he doesn't even believe that Jesus is alive again when his fellow disciples report their appearance encounter. He suspends judgment for an entire week until he touches Jesus' wounds and is convinced (Jn 20:24-29). I don't know if this is the only reason the risen Jesus isn't immediately recognized, but these stories all strongly hint that no one, not even his closest followers, expects to see him again after he is crucified.

Another mystery of the appearance stories is why the risen Jesus does not first appear to the disciples. Instead, the first to see the empty tomb and hear the announcement of Jesus' resurrection are women (Lk 24:1-10). The first explicit resurrection appearance is to Mary Magdalene (Jn 20:15-18). It is equally mysterious that Jesus' second resurrection appearance is to two obscure people on the Emmaus road who are mentioned nowhere other than in this passage (Lk 24:36-40). Why does Jesus appear to those on the fringe rather than the most inner of his inner circle? Honestly, I can't say for certain, but if we are getting used to God's sense of humor, it would not surprise me at all that he plans it this way. God uses the disempowered and overlooked woman to be the first to proclaim the resurrection of Jesus to those most closely linked with Jesus, and the inner circle passes it off as idle chit-chat. Two men who seem to be fringe Jesus-followers see Jesus and run back to tell the disciples about their encounter. It's a bit topsy-turvy, but God uses topsy-turvy a lot. Those who are the first proclaimers of Jesus' resurrection and the invasion of God's kingdom are the least expected. God does stuff like this, so it shouldn't surprise us that the first resurrection witnesses are surprising.

It might be sinful to play favorites, but I have to say that the Emmaus appearance story is particularly intriguing to me both because of Jesus' playfulness and the theological gravity of the story (Lk 24:13-35). The risen Jesus joins the two travelers on the way from Jerusalem back to Emmaus and inquires about their conversation. Cleopas asks him, incredulously, if he is the only one who hasn't heard about how Jesus had been handed over by the Jewish leaders for crucifixion and how on the third day the women had found the tomb empty. Wouldn't Jesus have chuckled at least a little since their perplexity is all about him? He is right there with them, and they have no clue who he is. Jesus' response is "Do tell." He's with them for several hours before there's any glimmer of recognition.

You cannot convince me that there is not a playful quality about this whole encounter, and I find it inconceivable that these two travelers wouldn't have told this story over and over again without a self-deprecating grin. They were with the risen Jesus for hours as he laid out the whole story of the Messiah from Moses to the present, and they didn't even recognize the star of the show until he broke the bread in their own house. The joke was on them, but as is the case with God's humor, the joke was for them. The one handed over to be crucified was *with* them, and they had no clue.

It is puzzling why Jesus chose to appear to Cleopas and his unnamed companion. Perhaps they were part of the seventy. Who knows? But once again, God brings the obscure and anonymous into his amazing story in a profound way. At the Last Supper, as Jesus breaks the bread and pours the wine, he says that he will not again drink the fruit of the vine "until the kingdom of God comes" (Lk 22:18). So when resurrected Jesus breaks the bread with the two from Emmaus, it is a birth announcement for the kingdom of God. This is huge, so a big public press conference seems logical. It's funny, God's style of funny, that two nobodies are the first witnesses and participants in the kingdom-of-God inaugural banquet.

EASTER ISN'T THE END OF IT, YOU KNOW

Baptists never make love standing up. They're afraid someone might see them and think they're dancing.

LEWIS GRIZZARD

I haven't told you the whole liturgical truth up to this point. From what I've said thus far, it looks like Easter is the single celebratory day that counterbalances the collective heaviness of Ash Wednesday, Lent, and Holy Week. But a quick glance at the liturgical calendar reveals a different story. Easter is followed by Eastertide. Eastertide is the un-Lent, a fifty-day celebration during which we bask in the light of redemption and new life. It is about feasting rather than fasting, thanksgiving for forgiveness rather than repentance of sin. If each Sunday is to be viewed as a weekly mini-Easter, Eastertide is to be observed as one massive fifty-day Sunday. Moreover, this season folds in two additional reasons to laugh and celebrate. It commemorates Jesus' ascension to the Father, the ultimate vindication of Jesus' identity and mission, and Pentecost, which brings the Holy Spirit and empowers God's adoptees to proclaim the good news "to the ends of the earth" (Acts 1:8). For those who are careful observers, we discover that Lent's extended period of fasting, repentance, and mourning is balanced with an even longer celebratory period.

Our quick look at the liturgical calendar is a visual reminder that there is "a time to weep, and a time to laugh; a time to mourn, and a time to dance" (Ecc 3:4). The Easter cycle reminds us that the proper times for weeping and laughter are intimately connected. They are not at opposite poles of the liturgical calendar but stand side by side. Yet when we compare the balance of repentance/sorrow and celebration/joy held in place by an Easter cycle that stretches from Ash Wednesday to Pentecost, it seems obvious that we are too often unbalanced in our own spiritual life. We have done a good job of developing a theology of suffering and death but have severely shortchanged the theological significance and centrality of laughter and dancing.

I know too many Christians who believe that the reason Jesus came to earth was to save us from dancing. However, it could revolutionize the church if instead we believed that Jesus came to save us *for* dancing. In view of Grizzard's statement, I'm not sure I really want to see a bunch of Baptists line dancing to "Achy Breaky Heart." However, I would like to hear them, and every other Christian in the world, occasionally doubled over in joyous laughter about God's victory over sin and death, his ascension to the Father, and the gift of the Holy Spirit. Check your liturgical calendar. There's a time for that.

IT WASN'T FUNNY THEN . . .

We have wilderness behind our house and bear visitations occur frequently enough that we had to get a bear-proof trashcan. Years ago, we had a basset hound named Flash (my appreciation for irony is not a new thing) who loved to chase the bears. It would scare me to death when this happened because I was worried that at some point in the pursuit, the bear was going to stop and think, "Wait a second, I'm three hundred pounds and he's eighty. He's slow and well-marbled and I'm an omnivore." Each time, though, the bear would disappear into the hills and Flash would waddle back, happy that he had once again kept the homestead safe from intruders.

"It wasn't funny when it happened, but we laugh about it now." We can all think of numerous occasions when we were in frustrating, awful, or dangerous situations that were anything that funny at the time. It wasn't funny when Flash the basset hound was out of sight in the hills. However, later, when he was home and safe, we looked back at the situation and laughed. The difference was distance. Time puts tragedy and fear into a broader perspective; it allows us to distance ourselves from the potential dangers of the immediate. Christianity provides an even wider panoramic temporal scope. We don't just see the past from the perspective of the present. God gives us eschatological distance, in which we can see the past and present through the lens of the future. This works because Easter is not just a day that happened slightly over two millennia ago; Easter is our future. Jesus was the "first fruits" of those who have been made alive by God, but we share in this at his future coming (1 Cor 15:23). Despite our own present mortality, we already know that Christ's present resurrection state is our future.

Eugene O'Neill wrote a play entitled *Lazarus Laughed,* which provides a fictionalized account of Lazarus's life after Jesus raised him from the dead (Jn 11:1-44). When summoned by Jesus to come out of the tomb, Lazarus emerges laughing, and continues to laugh uncontrollably throughout the play. Although death and sorrow fill the play— Jesus is crucified and Lazarus's parents, wife, children, and friends die— Lazarus continues to laugh and proclaim (in several variations):

> Laugh! Laugh!
> There is only God!
> Life is His Laughter.
> We are His Laughter.
> Fear is no more!
> Death is dead![4]

Lazarus's laughter continues even through his own second death, when he is burned alive by the crazy emperor, Caligula.

I think O'Neill's play gets it right, but the timing is off. Lazarus's restored life is best described as a resuscitation, not a resurrection. Earth is different from heaven. An age in which Lazarus's family dies and he is mercilessly tortured by an insane emperor is very different from another age in which "death will be no more; mourning and crying and pain will be no more" (Rev 21:4). Because death and suffering are still stubbornly entrenched in the world into which the raised Lazarus returns, to laugh without tears is to deny reality. Unbroken laughter is only appropriate when death itself, the last enemy, is destroyed (1 Cor 15:26) and God is "all in all" (1 Cor 15:28). A time is coming when we will laugh without interruption and can proclaim with O'Neill's Lazarus,

> Laugh! Laugh!
> There is only God!
> Life is His Laughter.
> We are His Laughter.
> Fear is no more!
> Death is dead!

But that time is not yet. Through eschatological distance, we gain a degree of separation from the pain, injustice, sordidness, and death of the current age. We can and should laugh in faith that Jesus' resurrection will also be ours. At the same time, our sin and death and the

---

[4]Eugene O'Neill, *Lazarus Laughed* (New York: Boni & Liveright, 1927), act 2, scene 2, http://gutenberg.net.au/ebooks04/0400131h.html.

world's ugliness are still real and weigh on us. There is so much that isn't funny right now, even if someday we'll be able to laugh about it.

Until the time when joy and laughter are uninterrupted, we will again begin the Easter cycle by listening to someone tell us on Ash Wednesday that we will eventually, maybe soon, become dust (Gen 3:19). With the exception of Good Friday, this may be the most brutal day of the church year because it confronts in a direct way the truth that we will die, decay into dust, and will be only minimally useful as fertilizer. As Lent continues, we will reflect on the depth of our sin and seek God's mercy. Holy Week will evoke mourning and tears as we relive the betrayal, torture, and death of Jesus. But just when our sorrow reaches crucifixion depths, we are abruptly snapped into a full celebratory mode by Easter and are warmed by the glow of ascension and Pentecost across a fifty-day feast time.

The Easter cycle is a humorous time because its awful lows and giddy highs seem so thoroughly incompatible. However, we cannot let go of either side of this dialectic. To ignore suffering and death is escapism; to lose resurrection hope and celebration plunges us into an Easter-denying despair. So we relive the Easter cycle every year. I'm suggesting, though, we should do it with a faint grin that reminds us that in God's now and our future, every day is Easter. We have heard God's life-giving punch line and realize this is God's joke for us.

INTERLUDE ONE

SARAH LAUGHED TWICE

> Even though the Bible doesn't tell us how old Isaac was when Abraham was called to sacrifice him, biblical scholars are certain he wasn't a teenager yet. Why? Because after they become teenagers, it's no longer a sacrifice.

Up to this point, I have generally used humor and laughter interchangeably. They are obviously closely related and for our purposes in most of this book, it is not too important to make a distinction. However, there is a difference. Humor, as we have noted, is the internal recognition of a tension in which worlds collide or when seemingly incompatible characters or events occupy the same space in surprising ways. Laughter is often, but not always, the external response when the tension of incongruities is released. It lets the air out of the balloon. I know, when explained, it seems to take the fun out of both humor and laughter.

We all experience stress, struggle, and tension in various forms, and laughter is one way we deal with it. And the relief we feel after a good laugh is the obvious answer to why we enjoy laughter and the humor that evokes it. However, we also seek the deflation of tension through laughter without humor. Nervous or embarrassed laughter is a way of disarming a stressful situation. Sarcastic laughter ironically signals that the anxiety we seek to dissipate through laughter still remains. Laughter occurs when we experience unexpected good fortune or see a loved one after a long absence. Tickling creates tension by the invasion of one's personal space and only results in laughter if one perceives "the tickling *as a mock attack*, a caress in a mildly aggressive disguise."[1] In short, laughing is a means by which we expel pent-up pressure.

Christians should be intimately aware of laughter as joyful release when prolonged disappointment and stress are resolved. After all, one of our most prominent family members, Isaac, whose very existence is the deflation of decades of yearning and frustration, is named "Laughter." And, as we know, biblical names are not incidental. They say something important about the name-bearer and about all those who are related.

When we hear Isaac's name, our mind immediately goes to the drama on Mount Moriah. Here, a father stands above his son with a knife and is prepared to sacrifice him. A danger here is that the idea of sacrifice tends to sanitize what seemed destined to occur. There is no sacrifice apart from killing. When Abraham is commanded to "take your son, your only son Isaac, whom you love" (Gen 22:2) and to kill him, he would do so not from the detached position of a high-altitude pilot dropping bombs from forty-three thousand feet, but face to face. This is an epic moment, properly so, and it brings us directly to questions—challenging and uncomfortable questions—about the nature of faith.

The story of Abraham's call to sacrifice Isaac deserves a central place in our narrative as a people, but I also worry that it overshadows what I increasingly find to be an equally and perhaps even more important faith lesson from Abraham. What does it mean to believe in God in the arduous, twisting, and often ambiguous decades-long journey that brought Abraham to the top of Mount Moriah with Isaac? It's easy to miss all of that because we read the Abraham story backwards, starting with the tension-deflating story of a ram caught in the thicket. Once this happens, we laugh with relief that Isaac's life is spared and that Abraham is spared from taking his son's life. But Abraham's life, like ours, is lived

---

[1]Arthur Koestler, *The Act of Creation* (London: Arkana, 1989), 80.

from beginning to end. Thus, the decades of unresolved struggles and uncertain outcomes that led to Mount Moriah cannot be forgotten.

THE LONG JOURNEY OF AN ELDERLY COUPLE

> Sarah: "Abraham, I'm okay with God talking to you and all that, but he's telling you to do some weird stuff. First, we have to raise the dead and try to make a baby with it. And now God told you to take a knife and cut part of it off? Are you sure you're hearing God right? You didn't get your hearing aid and your suppository mixed up again, did you?"
>
> Abraham looks up at Sarah, takes a suppository out of his ear, and says, "Huh?"

The story begins when God tabs Abraham, then names Abram, for no apparent reason, to be the father of a great nation (Gen 12:2). The pressure point is already there because the active ingredient of a great nation is a son. But Abram (age seventy-five) and his wife, Sarai (age sixty-five), are old and childless. When it comes to the potential for producing children, as Hebrews undiplomatically puts it, Abram was as "as good as dead" (Heb 11:12). Even his name, Abram, "Exalted Father," mocks him and amplifies the tension. Under normal circumstances, the promise of a son at this age goes beyond illogic; it seems like God is cruelly toying with Abram, and it only gets worse as year after year follows this promise.

Still, Abram leaves his home and his family and becomes a nomadic herdsman in a strange country. For him, there are the everyday stresses that come with running a family business, and the extraordinary stresses that come with the need to go to Egypt in order to find grazing lands (Gen 12:10), the separation with his nephew Lot to find sufficient feed for their herds (Gen 13:6), and the raid to rescue Lot when he has been taken captive by an invading army (Gen 14:12-16). Always in the background, though, is the emptiness. The promise of a son, unlikely at the beginning of the story, only becomes less likely as each day passes. However, Abram keeps going, with his pain, somehow believing even during all the years when God is silent.

God's silence is broken only infrequently during these many years. In one such disruption, Abram receives a vision from God that not only reaffirms the promise but makes it even more extravagant, and more painful given his present circumstances: his descendants will be as numerous as the stars (Gen 15:5-6). Another appearance of God to Abram occurs when he is ninety-nine years old. Abram is now renamed Abraham, "Father of Many" (Gen 17:5), as if his current name isn't sufficiently ironic and wrenching. Sarai (local or tribal princess) becomes Sarah ("Princess of All People")[2] (Gen 17:15).

LAUGHING IN DESPAIR/LAUGHING IN CELEBRATION

During her lecture, a noted linguist made the statement that there are several languages in which two negatives denote a positive (I can't not go = I have to go), but we know of no language in which two positives indicate a negative.

A voice from the back row said, "Yeah, right."

When God repeats the promise of a son, it seems that Abraham has finally reached his breaking point. He falls on the ground laughing! It's odd because he is not just laughing in God's presence, but it seems clear that it is a laughter of disbelief about what God tells him. As he lay on the ground laughing, he says to himself, "Will a son be born to a man a hundred years old? Will Sarah bear a child at the age of ninety" (Gen 17:17 NIV)?

---

[2]The Talmud states that for both name changes, the basic name remains the same, but the scope of Abraham's and Sarah's names is extended. "Abram the same is Abraham. At first he became a father to Aram [Ab-Aram] only, but in the end he became a father to the whole world. [Similarly] Sarai is the same as Sarah. At first she became a princess to her own people, but later she became a princess to all the world." Talmud, Berakoth, 13, www.halakhah.com/berakoth/berakoth_13.html.

These are rhetorical questions to which the expected answer is "Yeah, right. That's not going to happen." When speaking aloud to God, Abraham's disbelief comes out in his attempt to play the Ishmael card: "If only Ishmael might live under your blessing!" (Gen 17:18 NIV).

It is interesting that God doesn't rebuke Abraham for his laughing incredulity. But God doesn't make matters any easier from Abraham either. Despite the fact that the original promise seems even more distant and unattainable after all these years, God brings new urgency to the promise. God doubles down by telling Abraham that Ishmael is not the promised one. Instead, Sarah will bear a son within the year, and he is to be named Isaac (Gen 17:19-21). He also commands Abraham to prepare his clan to become people of the covenant by a sign that sets them apart: every male is to be circumcised. You either have to admire Abraham or deem him totally insane. In view of the unlikely prospects of a son at this stage of the couple's life and his disbelieving laughter moments before, it would seem more than a little crazy to subject every male in your entourage to the pain of circumcision (Gen 17:24-27). You have to believe there was a bit of grumbling about this.

Silence again follows, and the dull ache of childlessness continues. Then, Abraham gets another visit in which three mysterious visitors tell him that his wait is almost over; soon they will have a son (Gen 18:10). Sarah, eavesdropping on the visitors, also hears this promise and laughs a quiet but derisive laugh. Why wouldn't she? When the original promise was given, Sarah's biological clock was already counting down the fifth overtime, and twenty-five additional long years have only made God's vow seem even more absurd. So as she laughs, she also asks herself a question: "After I am worn out and my lord is old, will I now have this pleasure?" (Gen 18:12 NIV). Again, it's a rhetorical question to be answered with "Yeah, right."

Laughter tinged with bitterness is often our last line of defense in the midst of helplessness and disappointment. Not surprisingly, when one of the strangers confronts Sarah about her laughter, she lies (Gen 18:15). Had I been in her place, I too would have laughed, and I would have lied about it. After years of waiting, the promise now seems to be nothing less than a cruel joke. Surely this latest news feels like the dagger to her heart has been twisted. The stranger calls Sarah out on her lie, but interestingly, like Abraham, she is not rebuked for her laughter and the lack of belief that gives rise to it.

Ironically, grief and humor share the same roots. Both recognize a disjuncture between the way we believe the world should be and what actually is. Sarah knows that she should be a mother, and God has confirmed that this is indeed the ideal, but grief arises when her day-to-day world confronts her with a bleakly different reality. Thus, tears are often the response to this disjuncture, and no doubt Sarah has shed many over the years. However, as we see here, Sarah's laughter expresses the same emotions of frustration, despair, and grief that are generated by the dark gap between what is and what should be.

A year later, Sarah laughs a decidedly different laugh. Bitterness has been replaced by joy that borders on giddiness. The promised son has been born, and, as commanded, she and Abraham name him Isaac—"Laughter," or "He laughs." Laughter is the distinctly human response to reversal. Joyous laughter, like every aspect of God's salvation, is possible only by God's grace. So it just makes sense that, as daughters and sons of Abraham, every Christian bears the name of laughter. From the beginning, the story of God's people is rooted in a journey that starts in homelessness and helplessness and ends in the joyful, full-throated laughter that is possible only when God brings about the sort of reversal that is essential to humor's structure.

For all the daughters and sons of Sarah and Abraham, humor is the story about a couple of geezers who made a baby, with some help from God, of course. Laughter is the joy that comes with the release of the grief and desperation built up over years and decades of disappointment.

Thus, the capacity for comedy and laughter is not just coded into the human genome. It is essential to Christianity's DNA. When Sarah laughs with utter joy about God's plan for creating a people, she knows it is not just her private joke. For those who listen well to God's improbable plan, Sarah says of the birth, "everyone who hears will laugh with me" (Gen 21:6). Let joyful laughter ensue.

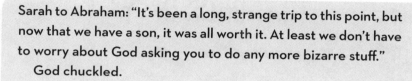

Sarah to Abraham: "It's been a long, strange trip to this point, but now that we have a son, it was all worth it. At least we don't have to worry about God asking you to do any more bizarre stuff."
God chuckled.

5

SEEING GOD ON TUESDAY, OR ANY OTHER DAY THAT ENDS IN "Y"

EXTRAORDINARY ORDINARY TIME

> Feeling the need for a spiritual recharge, a layperson checked into a monastery for a month-long retreat. After a monk showed him around the grounds and introduced him to his sparsely furnished cell, he said, "We hope you have a blessed time in our monastery. If you need anything, be sure to let one of the brothers know, and we will teach you how to do without it."

When we think of the spiritual life, the setting above often comes to mind. No job or family responsibilities, no cell phone or TV, and no creature comforts beyond our basic needs—although most won't go as far as taking a vow of celibacy. Some focused God-time is beneficial to all of us. However, most of our life does not pass in cloistered simplicity and focus but in the messiness of the everyday. So what should salvation look like in the day to day for ordinary Christians? Rather than assuming that the real action in Christianity is possible only when we are freed *from* the ordinary, is it possible that our salvation has room for the freedom *of* and freedom *for* the everyday?

The liturgical calendar designates two timespans—eight weeks after Christmastime and twenty-five weeks after Pentecost—as Ordinary

Time. This label arises from the word *ordinal,* which simply means "numbered" or "ordered." These two periods, comprising over 60 percent of the year, are not punctuated by high holy days, but contain the routines that are the stuff of life. The Christian's task during Ordinary Time is to recognize and enjoy God's small graces in the day to day. It is about finding God in the routine and the mundane and catching glimpses of the supernatural in the midst of what seems merely natural and ordinary. This is, of course, easier said than done. We have a good idea of the appropriate focus for our spiritual development during Advent and the Easter cycle. But how do we connect with God while spreading mulch or commuting to work? What does it mean to find a divine dimension in teaching a classroom of fourth-graders, comforting a colicky baby at 3 A.M., or wondering what your seventeen-year-old is really doing on a Saturday night? It's one thing to see God's hand extending into our world when something extraordinary happens and things "work out." However, it's another thing to discern God's involvement in the way things usually work. Is Ordinary Time also a holy time, or is it a period when we do the spiritual equivalent of treading water and counting down the days until the high holy seasons roll around again?

> *Jeff Allen on potty training their three-year-old:* My wife bought him one of the musical potty chairs. Have you seen these things? Every time he goes to the bathroom in it, it makes music. What kind of neurosis is this going to create? Thirty years from now he'll be laying on some shrink's couch. "You know, I just can't go to the restroom unless I'm wearing a Walkman. Doc, that elevator ride up just about killed me."
>
> JEFF ALLEN, "POOP BOY"—*HAPPY LIFE,*
> *HAPPY WIFE . . . REVISITED*

For most of us, humor is a welcome companion during Ordinary Time, and the ordinary features of life provide a fertile seedbed for humor. After all, most jokes are about the typical situations: food, bad hair, making ends meet, automotive malfunctions, doctor visits, husbands and wives, and trying to find just one of our eleven umbrellas when it finally rains. Even adventures in potty training a three-year-old are funny, or at least become so in hindsight. Laughter eases the stress and strain of life, and it also reminds us of the good in the everyday. The number of times we chuckle each day about what we find amusing in common events is a signal that our funny bone is a gift from God. However, I think there is much more to humor's role in everyday spirituality. It can be a tool that trains us to see the invisible, to imagine what is not immediately present to the senses, and to expect that we will find God in surprising places and ways.

> For a couple of years, I walked past a bookcase that contained, among other books, a familiar bestseller titled *How to Read a Book*. This is a common text on college campuses, so it didn't stand out at first.
>
> It finally hit me that this was an unusually large version of the book. One day I stopped, pulled it off the shelf, opened it up, and discovered that it was a copy of *How to Read a Book*—on tape.

For lovers of irony, you can't help but smile at the idea that you can learn how to read a book without actually, you know, reading a book. I had "seen" that object for years, but something happened that completely changed the way I now "see" it. Moreover, a new way of seeing this book caused me to contemplate other ways we might look at it. For example, I pondered, but only briefly, the market potential of piggybacking on the audio version of *How to Read a Book* by producing a movie titled *How to Listen to "How to Read a Book."*

As in humor, theology requires that we see something in our world that others do not, will not, or cannot see. This is certainly what Jesus has in mind when he refers to having ears that hear and eyes that see.

God was present and visible in the words and actions of Jesus, but only to those who were properly attuned. If not so attuned, spiritual deafness and blindness resulted. Stanley Hauerwas says that Christian ethics "is first a way of *seeing* before it is a matter of *doing*. The ethical task is not to tell you what is right or wrong but rather to train you to see."[1] This is true also of the Christian life in general.

When we think of spiritual development, we often contemplate the daily practices that bring us closer to God. This is certainly a worthy focus, but our practices need to be yoked with the ability to see. Thus, our emphasis will be on "spiritual optometry," the possibility of seeing God in an everyday world. To do this, we need to open ourselves to yet another humorous incongruity—the fact that God resides in the mundane and that the supernatural permeates the natural. We will also talk about some of the gifts God provides that allow us to see another dimension of reality.

FLATLAND

 The parallel lines had so much in common. Unfortunately, they never met.

It's not often you find a joke, let alone an entire novel, based on geometry, and for good reason. Surveys show that nine out of every eight people are just not very good at math. However, the novel *Flatland* (1884) assumes a bit of basic geometric knowledge and has been something of a cult classic (since math is a cult) for over a century. The book's narrator is A Square, a two-dimensional figure in a two-dimensional world, who visits the one-dimensional world of Lineland in a dream. When A Square attempts to convince Lineland's ruler that a

---

[1]Stanley Hauerwas and William H. Willimon, *Resident Aliens: A Provocative Christian Assessment of Culture and Ministry for People Who Know That Something Is Wrong* (Nashville: Abingdon Press, 1989), 95.

second dimension exists, he is threatened with death for advocating such a misguided and dangerous idea. Later, A Square meets A Sphere who, as you might guess, is a three-dimensional sphere. When A Sphere attempts to describe a 3-D universe, A Square is unable to grasp the concept of depth until he visits Spaceland and experiences it directly. Following this, the narrator tries to imagine a world that includes yet other dimensions, an idea that A Sphere rejects—roundly, of course.

What *Flatland* attempts to do in its own nerdy math way isn't dissimilar to one of the most common weapons in humor's arsenal. (Is it even legal to compare humor to math?) As noted before, humor often elicits laughter by seeing something that is present but unseen by others. Thus, the observation that we park on driveways and drive on parkways or that a simple space turns *therapist* into *the rapist* causes us to wonder why we didn't notice that earlier. Likewise, faith opens us to the possibility that God reveals himself in a realm where God is not immediately obvious.

Our brief visit to Flatland reveals a common obstacle for finding God in the everyday. We often are like the rulers of Lineland and Spaceland, beings who cannot imagine more dimensions of reality than our immediate experience offers. This lack of imagination has a number of causes, some of which we will consider in what follows. However, one fundamental problem is simply stunted expectation. We have become so familiar with the 3-D world of our senses that we don't really expect to find another dimension of reality. Still, there is good reason to believe that hints of God's presence have been tucked into the world we experience with our five senses, if we have expectant eyes that see.

A GOD-ODD WORLD

Never been able to get out of a speeding ticket? Try this next time. When you are pulled over for going 80 mph in a 60-mph zone, politely point out to the officer that you would only have been speeding only if our planet was stationary. However, since Earth moves at 67,000 mph, your actual cosmic speed was negative since you were driving in a direction opposite that of the Earth's orbit.

Of course, the downside to this is you might receive a ticket for driving 66,920 mph in reverse, and the fine for that would likely be larger than one for going 20 mph over the speed limit while moving forward.

To open ourselves to perceiving God in natural processes and everyday life, it helps to remember that we already believe things about our world that seem too outrageous to be true. As this joke correctly notes, planet Earth is hurtling through space at 67,000 miles per hour (and spinning at the rate of about one thousand miles per hour) despite the fact that we don't feel like we are in motion at all. Thus, we earthlings are simultaneously ordinary folks who walk at an average pace of four miles per hour and space travelers moving at almost one hundred times the speed of sound while sitting in our recliner. Physics tells us that walls are mostly empty space filled with tiny bits of rapidly moving matter. On one level, this information makes no sense, especially if you are trying to run through the wall. Still, we believe, and with good reason, that there is more to this strange universe than can be detected by the naked eye. The wonder and mystery of our world should remind us that there are dimensions of reality that our eyes do not see.

There's nothing better on a hot day than a tall glass of ice water. Unfortunately, as the ice melts, it dilutes my water and I have to start all over again.

I keep seeing drinks in the store advertised as "enhanced water." Isn't everything we drink water that has been enhanced in some way?

The oddness of the universe is not confined to the faraway heavens. It is as close as one of the most fundamental necessities of life: water. As good as water is in its most basic form (as long as it isn't diluted), our enjoyment of life is heightened by various enhancements of water. One way to accomplish this is by adding flavorings and other elements to it. Even when we don't have a direct hand in water enhancement, plants, hydrated by the rain, add flavor and nourishment. This results in beverages such as grape juice, which is essentially water enhanced by natural processes. Of course, the Christian believes that the world is not simply odd. It's a God-odd place in which God engineered the "natural" processes by which water is transformed into grape juice. For those who enjoy the additional enhancement of fermentation (Episcopalians call it the "second blessing"), God created that process as well. The wedding at Cana (Jn 2:1-11) is not the first time God turned water into wine. God does it all the time, whether or not the people at Gallo acknowledge his role. And if we can see God's hand in what we typically think of as the natural processes of growth and fermentation, it is no less miraculous than when Jesus skips a few steps by transforming water directly into wine at Cana.

All this goes beyond the beverage aisle at the grocery store. Our own bodies are essentially "enhanced water." Fifty to 70 percent of our weight is water. So if you insist that you have a water retention issue rather than a weight problem, it turns out that they are pretty much the same thing. If you add nitrogen and carbon to the oxygen and hydrogen, these four elements alone account for 96 percent of our body's composition. This is more or less true of our food as well. So there is more than a little truth in the well-known statement, "You are what you eat." But behind all the chemistry, there is a mystery: somehow inert stuff from the periodic table of elements becomes alive, sustains our life, and is tasty to boot. Thanks be to God indeed.

IT'S ONLY FUNNY BECAUSE IT'S TRUE

Have you ever noticed that fundraisers rarely play to the strengths of the groups for whom funds are being raised? An ultramarathon to raise money to fight childhood obesity? There isn't an obvious tie-in between the activity and the beneficiaries. Girl Scouts are much more adept at cookie consumption than cookie sales.

For me, though, the strangest fundraiser is the marching-band car wash. Is there anything about marching in formation while playing a musical instrument that translates into car-washing skills? Yet statistics show that 83 percent of all cars in this country have been washed by a high school percussion section.

It's not even clear why marching bands were created, other than the need to kill fifteen minutes in the middle of a football game. I've never heard anyone claim that walking rhythmically and making mechanical gestures while playing music prepares you for the job market. In fact, watching marching bands is probably where someone came up with the idea of replacing the human workforce with robots.

As far as I can tell, there is only one good reason to have a kid play a sousaphone, dress in a hideous uniform, play mid-nineteenth-century military music while forming the letter "S" between the 40- and 50-yard lines with the trombone section, and spend every weekend doing car washes—this combination of factors greatly decreases the odds that they will use drugs. The marching band doesn't need drugs. Their world is weird enough already.

Have you ever noticed that so many standup routines, like the one above, start with the question: "Have you ever noticed?" Observational humor is one of my favorite genres because it sees the funny in what is familiar and mundane. You don't have to explain to anyone what a marching band is or does. Nevertheless, observational humor notices something that, up to this point, had flown under the radar of our consciousness. Marching-band car washes are common, but now we stop and ask why. What is the connection?

One reason observational humor is so popular is that it deals with the ordinary and mundane, but it hands it back to us as something surprising, new, and bigger. Laughter is a sign of our delight in seeing something with new eyes. Moreover, once we have seen the old and familiar in a new way, we can't "unsee" it. So you may have a hard time driving past a parking lot where a band is holding a car wash without smiling a little bit.

Likewise, if we have ever noticed the incredible possibilities God invests in something as simple as water, we can never see it in the same way. A marching-band car wash begins with the cleansing properties of water, but there is much more going on than that. This is especially the case when we remember that baptism—our holy-water bath—is the vehicle that marks our cleansing from sin and signals our inclusion into the people of God. And our confession that Jesus is present to us in the Eucharist's water-enhanced-to-become-wine (fermented or not) should be a hint that God may be perceived in some other rather ordinary and visible things, and even in some ordinary things we can't see.

THE INVISIBLE WITHIN THE VISIBLE

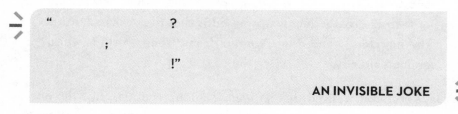

"

?

;

!"

AN INVISIBLE JOKE

Invisibility fascinates us, and I doubt that a human has ever existed who did not wish at some time that they had the power of invisibility. Our physical and visible bodies are a constant reminder of our limitations and finitude, so we are drawn to superpowers like invisibility that would allow us to transcend some of the constraints of embodiment and render us more godlike. While invisibility fascinates, it also frustrates. People have long proclaimed that our inability to see God is a barrier to belief. Even Christians get in on this game, arguing that God's invisibility makes it difficult to find a sense of relationship with him.

Frustration with God's invisibility is ironic for a couple of reasons. First, we would not find a god who was visible to the naked eye to be much of a god, especially if this god looked like a manatee. In addition, the list of invisible things we have no trouble believing in is pretty long: time, heat, magnetism, radio waves, dark matter, radiation, and electricity, to name just a few. People don't doubt the existence of the number 40, which is a real and useful but invisible cognitive concept we represent with visible symbols like "XL" (which makes sense since this is about the age I started requiring clothes that had XL on the tag).

At this point, we find another oddity about our existence. On the one hand, we are physical beings endowed with optical organs that see only material objects. On the other hand, we have other powers that allow us to see, understand, and use invisible forces. If this is the case, we don't just have the visual powers of a duck or wolf; we have superpowers. Maybe we can't become invisible, although some people can disappear when it is time to do dishes, but we can do something even more impressive. We can see the invisible.

HUMAN SUPERPOWERS

René Descartes was sitting in a bar and drinking a beer, thoughtfully, of course. When he had finished, the bartender asked if he wanted another. Descartes said, "I think not," and immediately disappeared from sight.

Descartes's famous dictum, "I think, therefore I am," is his tribute to the amazing power of reason. Reason is a way of seeing and knowing the truth about realities that lack visual qualities. Thus, we often say, "Oh, I see," when we finally grasp the solution to a complex problem. And intellectual eyesight allows us to see the sorts of invisible things just mentioned. We have an understanding of how magnetism and gravity work because of rationality. The capacity for deductive thought helps us get through algebra class and balance the checkbook. Moreover, we had better think carefully about how we wire that light switch because what you can't see (for example, electricity) can kill you.

Reason is so widespread that we don't usually think of it as a superpower. However, how likely does it seem that the order and logic in our cosmos originates from the materials and energies of the universe itself? Instead, it seems more probable that something akin to a Mind is behind its laws and regularities. And if our minds are capable of reading this cosmic Mind, that is a superpower. In addition, Christians throughout history have understood that there is something supernatural about our ability to get beyond visible, changing, and temporary things to contemplate the invisible, the eternal, and the unchanging. Indeed, if rationality is one of God's attributes, reason is one way we operate on a divine wavelength. Christians are not alone in this belief. Plato says that we can see divine realities because we are not just meat and bone, but possess the power to see the invisible because we have an invisible, rational soul that participates in some way with the divine. Aristotle also refers to reason as the highest capacity of humans, and that which makes us most godlike.[2]

---

[2]"Now he who exercises his reason and cultivates it seems to be both in the best state of mind and most dear to the gods. For if the gods have any care for human affairs . . . it would be reasonable both that they should delight in that which was best and most akin to them (i.e., reason) and that they should reward those who love and honor this most, as caring for the things that are dear to them." Aristotle, *Nicomachean Ethics*, in *The Basic Works of Aristotle*, ed. Richard McKeon (New York: Random House, 1941), 1179a.

Two cows are standing in the field. One asks the other, "Are you worried about this mad cow disease going around?" The other replies, "Why should I be? I'm a helicopter."

On one level, this joke is just silly. At the same time, it is a good illustration of the intellectual nature of humor. In order to get the joke, we depend on reason to do two things: First, it provides information about the symptoms of mad cow disease, and then it deduces that the neurological damage caused by the disease is the reason the second bovine believes it is a helicopter. Again, as humor so often does, it brings two worlds together. In one world, science identifies the causes of mad cow disease; in another world, bovines chat and self-identify as helicopters. Our laughter at the joke is a celebration of our intellect. In that brief time gap between the end of the joke and when our mind brings these two worlds together in such a way that we get it, we are in a state of thought. "Getting it" is reason solving a problem—understanding the truth of the situation—and laughter is our reward for doing so correctly.

In a similar way, good science and good theology share a common task. Both rely on reason to bring two worlds together. We have become so comfortable with these intersections of the visible and the invisible that we don't really think about how odd it is that my cell phone can snatch unseen radio signals out of the air or that electricity can power a huge motor. Yet our rational superpower helps us understand how these two very different dimensions work together.

While science tends to limit itself to using reason as a tool for discovering the truth about our universe, theology wants to know a little bit more. Why does this bond between the tangible and intangible even exist? Why is the universe intelligible to reason, even if only partly so, and what does it ultimately mean? I think James Schall gets it right: "The universe does not exist just to be there, it exists to be known. And once it is known, it exists that its knower within it might achieve his own end which, at bottom, consists in knowing the knower of its whole order of things."[3] This means that if we push deep enough with our understanding of reason, merely secular learning is impossible. Reason helps reveal the means by which God governs his creation and how we might best live within it.

SEEING GOOD WELL

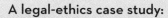

A legal-ethics case study:

A lawyer was approached by an acquaintance who said he would give her a $100 bill if she would answer a five-minute legal question. She agreed, and after she answered his inquiry, as promised, she received a $100 bill. Later, she realized that her friend had accidentally given her two $100 bills that were stuck to each other.

The ethical dilemma: Does she tell her law partners about the extra $100 bill?

While the list of invisible realities our reason discerns is extensive, there is an additional superpower that joins forces with reason and allows us to see another invisible dimension. Our moral sensibility allows us a glimpse into the realm of goodness. Humor is a part of our superpower package that teams up with moral sensibility. When we process this joke, our moral superpower reminds us that we have ethical duties. Since we all have experienced the temptation to keep what is not ours, we naturally assume that the ethical dilemma is whether to give the money back to the client who accidentally overpaid (as if that should even be a dilemma). Thus, we may not even recognize it as a joke until the twist at the end in which our typical ethical expectations are torpedoed.

---

[3] James V. Schall, "On *The Universe We Think In*," *Law and Liberty*, June 19, 2018, www.liberty lawsite.org/2018/06/19/on-the-universe-we-think-in-schall-what-is/.

As with reason, you might think that moral judgment is quite ordinary since humans engage in such evaluations throughout each day. However, it is quite extraordinary in the sense that it allows us to see the invisible in two different ways. First, as noted, to say that moral goodness demands that we should return property to its rightful owner is a claim to see a reality—goodness—that lacks weight, mass, color, or any other sensory property. Second, to say, "The lawyer *ought* to return the extra $100 bill to its rightful owner," involves seeing the future. What ought to happen is "seen" even though it hasn't yet occurred. Our moral sense makes us time travelers.

Another reason we should not dismiss our moral sense's superpower status is that other superpowers—time travel, the ability to fly, or the capacity to untie another person's shoes by wiggling your ears—do not have sufficient power to make us good people. In fact, the temptation to misuse invisibility for unethical purposes would be almost overwhelming, something recognized in literature from Plato's "Ring of Gyges"[4] to H. G. Wells's *Invisible Man*. By contrast, proper use of our moral superpower allows us to be more godlike since, after all, God is more than just powerful. God is good. In my book, this makes our capacity for moral judgment and action a superpower.

BEHOLDING BEAUTY

 Yo mama's so ugly that when she signed up for an ugly contest, they said, "Sorry, no professionals."

I'm reasonably certain that one of the reasons we enjoy pets so much is that they lack aesthetic judgment. They just don't care if Mama is homely and dumpy as long as she feeds and pets them. Humans, however, recognize and crave the beautiful, and the ability to make

---

[4]Plato, *Republic* 2.359a-360d.

judgments about beauty is one of our superpowers. While we most often think of beauty in a visual sense, it can be properly applied to a wide variety of experiences. Physicists describe a theory as beautiful, just as we might refer to a wise solution to an everyday problem with the same word. Some people have lovely personalities. The arc of a perfectly struck nine-iron is a thing of beauty and, for me, rare. Beauty is perceived by all humans in a variety of forms, yet it is mystery. What do all these have in common? Perhaps Aquinas offers the best definition available when he says, "Beautiful things are those which please when perceived."[5]

> The basic chords [in Renaissance music] were the ones we still have with us, the triads, the major one, which we think is happy, and the minor one, which we perceive as sad. But what's the actual difference between these two chords? It's just these two notes in the middle. It's either E-natural, at 659 vibrations per second, or E-flat, at 622. So the big difference between human happiness and sadness? Thirty-seven freakin' vibrations.
>
> **MICHAEL TILSON THOMAS[6]**

Our experience of musical beauty offers a wonderful example of the intersection between the physical and the transcendent. The music that stirs our souls and excites our emotions emanates from instruments made of wood, metal, skin, and electronic circuits in concert with our breath and the movements of our extremities. The various pitches can be reduced to numbers of vibrations per second, but we know that music's beauty transcends the movements of air. One can have a deep knowledge of sonic theory, understanding how vibrations from vocal

---

[5] Aquinas, *Summa Theologiae*, I, 5, iv, ad. 1. The word *perceived* here means more than just experienced visually. It refers to a recognition of beauty in any of the forms mentioned above.
[6] Michael Tilson Thomas, "Music and Emotion Through Time," TED: Ideas Worth Spreading, TED 2012, www.ted.com/talks/michael_tilson_thomas_music_and_emotion_through_time/transcript.

cords or cello strings create movements in the air, setting into motion the vibrations in our eardrums that, in turn, cause electrical-chemical signals in our brains. Somehow, this becomes music. If anything, this intensifies our musical experience because, regardless of the depth of our knowledge of sonic theory, we still don't understand how pulsating eardrums or neurological sequences are translated into beauty.

Whether we perceive beauty and experience its pleasure in the innocence of a child or in a dazzling sunset, it unifies the natural and supernatural dimensions of our being. The capacities to discern and respond to it are deeply embodied, yet our judgments about beauty are not reducible to bodily operations. Similarly, beauty is often found in perceptible objects or bodies, but the beauty of such things cannot be equated with some part, color, or weight. Because of the irreducibility of beauty, it requires a spectacular superpower to discern. This is why Christians throughout history have proclaimed that the perception of beauty is only possible when we find hints of a beautiful God in the world that operate on the same frequency as our aesthetic superpower.

THE TRANSCENDENTALS

I'm far from the first to think of reason, moral sense, and aesthetic capacity as superpowers, although most thinkers are too classy to refer to them by a word that frequently shows up in comic books. Still, so many of history's great intellects argue that our ordinary extraordinary abilities point to what they called the transcendentals—the True, the Good, and the Beautiful. And the Christians within this group will tell us that these realities are embedded in creation because the Creator is the source and perfection of all that is true, good, and beautiful.[7]

---

[7]Some Christians view the transcendentals as a reflection of the Trinity, arguing that where there is truth, there is also goodness and beauty. See Peter Kreeft, "Lewis's Philosophy of Truth, Goodness, and Beauty," in *C. S. Lewis as Philosopher: Truth, Goodness, and Beauty*, ed. David Baggett, Gary R. Habermas, and Jerry L. Walls (Downers Grove, IL: IVP Academic, 2008), 25-26.

These transcendentals (which would be a great label for a band of superheroes) are so named for a number of reasons. First, as noted before, our ability to discern these realities surpasses what we can account for simply by taking an inventory of our bodily functions. Animals and humans have similar sensory abilities, some of which surpass the acuity of our own, and our brains function in much the same way that a critter's will. Our genome is strikingly similar to that possessed by primates. Yet we don't rely on orangutans to write calculus textbooks, design a museum, or determine whether it is morally permissible to remove Aunt Mabel's feeding tube. Thus, the superpowers that allow us to see the invisible set us apart from other animals and represent our highest functions.[8]

Second, we call these realities transcendent since any particular instance of goodness, truth, or beauty is partial and imperfect. However, each partial and imperfect example seems to point beyond itself toward goodness, truth, or beauty itself. After all, how would we recognize a specific instance of moral goodness as good unless we had a general concept of goodness?

Finally, many Christians think of these as transcendentals since they are designed to point us toward the transcendent one who is their source—God. Where else would such wonderful and powerful gifts come from? If these common, very human superpowers give us such capacities, it follows that, if we have eyes to see, wherever we discern truth, goodness, or beauty we see the activity of God.[9] And since these abilities can take us to God, even in the midst of what seems merely mundane and commonplace, they are spiritual superpowers.

---

[8]As the *Catechism of the Catholic Church* says, "The manifold perfections of creatures—their truth, their goodness, their beauty—all reflect the infinite perfection of God." *Catechism of the Catholic Church*, I, 1, 1, IV, 41, www.vatican.va/archive/ENG0015/__PC.HTM.

[9]We should note that these transcendentals find close parallels in Philippians 4:8 (NIV): "Finally, brothers and sisters, whatever is true, whatever is noble, whatever is right, whatever is pure, whatever is lovely, whatever is admirable—if anything is excellent or praiseworthy—think about such things."

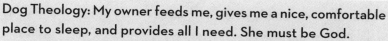

> Dog Theology: My owner feeds me, gives me a nice, comfortable place to sleep, and provides all I need. She must be God.
>
> Cat Theology: My owner feeds me, gives me a nice, comfortable place to sleep, and provides all I need. I must be God.

Some things can be either visible or invisible under differing circumstances. Stars can't be seen during daylight. Apparently, shoes become invisible to humans during adolescence. Certain things become visible under ultraviolet light, so a black light will reveal where your cat has been urinating. You could also just ask your cat to point out all its favorite pee spots since felines probably see in ultraviolet.[10] But given their self-perceived sense of divinity, your cat probably doesn't think it owes you that courtesy. The sad reality is that, even though we possess superpowers that allow us to see God, there are certain conditions that cause us to lose this ability.

Power in all its forms can be either useful or dangerous, and this becomes even more true when power is supersized. Movies are populated with evil geniuses who endeavor to use their superhuman abilities to bring death, destruction, and domination. In a similar way, because our superpowers are spiritual in nature, they lead to spiritual destruction when they become perverse. Thus, our spiritual superpowers, when rightly deployed, allow us to see the highest of all invisible realities in the midst of our ordinary lives. Ironically, however, these abilities that allow us to see the invisible lead to spiritual blindness when misused, a lesson Balaam learned the hard way.

> An elderly man was taking a stroll through the forest when he happened upon a frog on the path. When he knelt down to pick up the frog, it said to him, "I am a beautiful princess who has been cursed by an evil witch. If you kiss me, the hex will be broken, and I will be your princess forever."

---

[10]Tanya Lewis, "Cats and Dogs May See in Ultraviolet," *Live Science*, February 18, 2014, www .livescience.com/43461-cats-and-dogs-see-in-ultraviolet.html.

> The old man simply held the frog-princess and continued his walk. After some time, the frog asked, "Didn't you hear me? If you kiss me, my beauty will be restored, and I will be at your service."
>
> "I heard you," the man said, "but at my age, a talking frog seems a lot more interesting."

I suspect that we like stories and jokes with talking animals because we would really like to know what they're thinking. If you've read Numbers recently (and who hasn't?), you know that Shrek isn't the first famous character with a talking donkey. Balaam had one too, and Balaam's donkey (Num 22:21-41), like Shrek's, isn't shy about telling her owner what's on her mind.

Balaam was a prophet of Baal who sold his services to the highest bidder. Balak, Israel's enemy, was worried about an Israelite population boom. So Balak offered Balaam all sorts of goodies to curse Israel so he could defeat them before they became too powerful. God warned Balaam against doing this, but Balaam pushed forward anyway. As he was on his way to meet Balak, God put an angry angel with a sword in Balaam's path, ready to do in this prophet. Balaam, who marketed himself as one "who sees the vision of the Almighty" (Num 24:16), is nevertheless unable to see this threat, even though the sword-swinging angel is clearly visible to the she-ass[11] on which he is riding. Three times the donkey avoids the threatening angel, and three times Balaam abuses her even though she has saved him from death (Num 22:22-35). A donkey who sees better than a seer is funny, but it gets even funnier when the ass lets the mighty prophet have it for beating her while she's saving his sorry, uh, donkey.

GENERAL REVELATION

What I've been talking about in this chapter has a fancy theological name: general revelation. This refers to the ways God reveals himself

---

[11]It is unclear why the text specifies that the donkey was female. Perhaps he-ass is redundant.

118

to all people through creation and our inner selves. Christians broadly agree that God photobombs creation, and the superpowers were intended to allow us to see God in the picture. As Paul puts it, "Ever since the creation of the world his eternal power and divine nature, invisible though they are, have been understood and seen through the things he has made" (Rom 1:20; see also Ps 19:1-4). The bad news is that sin exerts a negative impact on these powers. They don't go away. Instead, they become twisted in a perversely ironic way. The superpowers are so deeply implanted in us that we cannot be irreligious. We can't not worship. Instead, we worship other gods, idols, ourselves, or the superpowers themselves. Paul states it like this: We "exchanged the truth about God for a lie and worshiped and served the creature rather than the Creator" (Rom 1:25).

Some Christians argue that sin's damage was so great that our superpowers can do nothing to lead us toward regeneration, while others say that with God's prevenient grace, our God-given superpowers can lead us back toward salvation. However, the majority of the world's Christians agree that when God has restored us to a relationship with him, these abilities, focused through the lens of Scripture, can help us once again see God within the created order.

> A psychoanalyst shows a patient an inkblot and asks him what he sees. The patient says, "A man and woman making love." The psychoanalyst shows him a second inkblot, and the patient says, "That's also a man and woman making love." The psychoanalyst says, "You are obsessed with sex." The patient explodes: "What do you mean I'm obsessed? You're the one with all the dirty pictures!"

I'm convinced that many of us blame God for something that is our fault, something that this psychoanalyst might call projection. We don't see God clearly and consistently when we look at creation, so we assume that God is like an absentee landlord who drops in only on rare occasions. But what if God is not just present in every fold and corner of the universe? What if God speaks to us in what brings delight, which seems exactly the way we would expect a kind and loving God to speak? Proverbs 8 makes me believe this is likely the case. Here, Wisdom describes herself as the first act of creation and as present with God in the subsequent stages of creation:

> When he [God] marked out the foundations of the earth,
> then I [Wisdom] was beside him, like a master worker;
> and I was daily his delight,
> rejoicing before him always,
> rejoicing in his inhabited world
> and delighting in the human race. (Prov 8:29-31)

In a similar passage, God tells Job that as he establishes "the foundation of the earth," the "heavenly beings shouted for joy" (Job 38:4-7).

If the response of God's wisdom and God's angels to creation and the human race is joy and delight, it seems logical that we should look for God's fingerprints within creation in the things that evoke delight. Calvin wrote in the *Institutes,* "nor was it ever forbidden to laugh, or to be full . . . or to be delighted with music, or to drink wine."[12] Look, if it's all right for Calvinists to laugh, enjoy food and drink, and take pleasure in music, it has to be allowable for Christians of all kinds.

Christians have often been suspicious of pleasure and delight. Rightly so, because, as is the case for our superpowers, God's gifts can be misused. But have we stopped to notice that so many of the elements necessary to sustain life are also enjoyable? It doesn't have to be this way. Taking a shower might cause great pain, and eating might be the most unpleasant thing we have to do, but it's quite the opposite. I'm willing to guess that the pleasurable element in each is intended to be a divine hint of another dimension, although I haven't figured out how

---

[12]John Calvin, *The Institutes of the Christian Religion,* trans. Henry Beveridge (Edinburgh, 1845), III.19.9, www.ccel.org/ccel/calvin/institutes/.

Brussels sprouts works into all this yet. Still, I suspect that we are more right than we know when we describe a warm chocolate-chip cookie or a hot shower as heavenly. We might find that the delight experienced by Wisdom and the angels in the created order is the sign of a generous God who wants us to praise him because of all that is good.

EATING

> Of course what makes breakfast in bed so special is you're lying down and eating bacon, the most beautiful thing on earth. Bacon's the best. Even the frying of bacon sounds like an applause. (*Sizzling sounds.*) Yeah, bacon! You wanna hear how good bacon is? To improve other food they wrap it in bacon. If it wasn't for bacon we wouldn't even know what a water chestnut is. "Thank you, bacon. Sincerely, Water Chestnut the Third." And those bits of bacon. Bits of bacon are like the fairy dust of the food community.
>
> **JIM GAFFIGAN, "BACON,"** *KING BABY*

Other than sex, eating is probably the most common theme in standup, with overeating constituting a significant subtheme within the genre. In many ways, it vividly illustrates both the possibility of finding God in the common as well as the potential to misuse a divine gift. Like Jim Gaffigan, I experience great delight in bacon consumption, as well as the consumption of just about anything else that's edible. Yet, when we look at the different dimensions of our life, the word *temptation* is most likely to be used in connection with food. In fact, gluttony is perhaps the only one of the seven deadly sins we willingly own up to. We hear a lot about eating disorders, but not nearly enough about disordered eating in which yummy elements within God's creation are treated merely as a means to our own selfish goals.

Yet when Paul tells us, "Whether you eat or drink, or whatever you do [*note*: "whatever you do" is pretty inclusive], do everything for the

121

glory of God" (1 Cor 10:31), it seems that those who have eyes to see should find theological significance in every activity, no matter how mundane. As a starter, the need for food tells us an uncomfortable truth about ourselves. As I bowed my head to pray before a meal one day, I realized in a new way something that is blatantly obvious: if I don't eat, I will die. It won't happen if I miss the next meal, or even several more next meals. I have, after all, built up a significant reserve. But I am finite and will eventually require refueling. I can look at my plate and see meatloaf, carrots, and garlic toast as tasty commodities that I paid for and thus can use as I please. Or I can see the goodness of a God who does not just supply what I need to prolong my life but also makes it pleasurable. If I look a little further, I can see God's work in all the good things that can and should happen around food, whether it is the strengthening of family bonds as we recount the day's events or the creation of friendships around a table. Done rightly then, eating provides some of us five or six opportunities to glorify God daily.

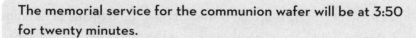

> The memorial service for the communion wafer will be at 3:50 for twenty minutes.

I'm not a big fan of looking for the face of Jesus in a waffle cone or pita bread. I do think, however, that we should see the work of God in what we eat, and there's a certain meal—the Lord's Supper—that convinces me of this. You can buy communion wafers on Amazon. On one level, it is ironic that the body of Christ can be purchased by credit card from the archetypical symbol of consumerism and sent to your church by next-day shipping. For high-maintenance congregations, you can get gluten-free, kosher (yes, really), organic communion bread. Most varieties of wafers, however, contain quite basic ingredients—wheat flour, water, shortening, salt—the same ingredients you find in a hot-dog bun. Maybe this is one way God delights in his creation. He hides himself within bread, one of the most basic and universal foods, but in such a way that those who have God-eyes see him clearly. On one level, we see nothing but the same sort of food we consume every day. At the same time, it is also the meal that brings us to God's throne and primes us for the ultimate celebration, the marriage feast of Christ and his bride (Rev 19:6-9), the greatest Happy Meal ever.

UNDERSTATEMENTS

"'Tis but a scratch." (*The Dark Knight's response to King Arthur cutting off his arm in a sword fight.*)

"Just a flesh wound." (*The Dark Knight's response to King Arthur cutting off his other arm.*)

MONTY PYTHON AND THE HOLY GRAIL

Humor often uses understatement as a tool. British humor, as exemplified by these Monty Python lines, is well known for this, but even Americans can get in on the understatement game. One line that shows up on almost every list of memorable movie quotes comes from the character Brody, played by Roy Scheider, in *Jaws*. After seeing the enormous shark, he says simply, "We're going to need a bigger boat." It isn't immediately clear what's funny about this. What Brody says is obvious. However, the viewer knows it shouldn't be interpreted as a straight line. The humor arises because, even while telling the truth, "We're going to need a bigger boat" downplays the actual situation to the extent that it seems to lose contact with reality. A severed arm *is* technically a flesh wound, but it far surpasses the seriousness of "just" a flesh wound.

Here's my contribution to understatement: if God is to be found in Ordinary Time, we are going to need a bigger world. We will, of course, have vital need for all that is ordinary, familiar, and sometimes boring in the world apparent to our senses. Parental duties, laundry, friendships, and termites will still be there. However, as the great philosopher

Yogi Berra once said, "You can observe a lot just by watching." Likewise, with the extraordinary superpowers God has bestowed on us and has redeemed, we can observe hints of the divine in the ordinary if we live with watchful expectation.

> People keep telling me that I should live each day as if it is my last. So I hopped into a hospital bed, since chances are good that this is where I'll spend my last day. I started an IV drip with a heavy dose of morphine-based painkillers, went into a coma, and listened to what everyone in my room said about me when they thought I couldn't hear anything. All in all, not a bad day, but I'm not convinced that is how I should live every day of my life.

Linguists tell us that "the process of reacting to and appreciating humor begins with the activation of a script in the brain's temporal lobes."[13] A script consists of our brain's expectations for the future based on past experiences. So when we think about what we want the last day of our life to be like, we construct a script from delightful and mean-ingful experiences of the past, such as spending time with family and beloved friends, surveying a spectacular vista, and eating our favorite meal. Humor happens when reality goes off-script and disrupts expec-tations with a quite different last-day-of-life scenario. This parallels what happens when we find fragments of heaven sprinkled throughout the everyday. We expect to find the ordinary events of everyday life, but occasionally God peeks out through an interaction with a coworker or a brief choking event in which we recognize the blessing of breath. The tension between the holy and the mundane maintains both, so if we have eyes to see, we keep discerning things that seem to be out of place.

Humor catches our attention because it anticipates a surprise. If my prior joke begins with a cue that the goal is comedic, you won't expect

---

[13]Richard Restak, "Laughter and the Brain," *The American Scholar*, June 10, 2013, https://theamerican scholar.org/laughter-and-the-brain.

that thoughtful meditation on my final day on earth will follow, even if the joke-teller's tone seems to fit such a contemplation. You don't know where it's leading you, but you're sure there will be a twist. You just don't know what it is yet. And it is during the time between the setup and the punch line that wonder and imagination kick into gear, trying to anticipate where the "script" will be disrupted by the unexpected.

The sense of anticipation that makes humor pleasurable parallels the mechanics of everyday spirituality. Faith expects that God will do surprising things and pop up in unexpected places. Cooking dinner, washing the car, or tying shoes are not the sorts of activities that seem to lend themselves to spiritual insight. But we know that God goes off-script and surprises us in unlikely ways. If we view God as a playful jokester, we don't know for sure where or how it will happen. We just know that we will be pleasantly surprised by the punch line.

TWO CALENDARS

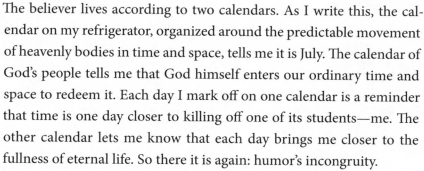

Time is a great teacher. Unfortunately, it kills all its students.

The believer lives according to two calendars. As I write this, the calendar on my refrigerator, organized around the predictable movement of heavenly bodies in time and space, tells me it is July. The calendar of God's people tells me that God himself enters our ordinary time and space to redeem it. Each day I mark off on one calendar is a reminder that time is one day closer to killing off one of its students—me. The other calendar lets me know that each day brings me closer to the fullness of eternal life. So there it is again: humor's incongruity.

We worship with God's people Sunday morning and watch football that afternoon. We pass out candy to masked extortionists on Halloween and acknowledge our kinship with believers who have passed into eternal life on All Saints' Day. We mark our calendars for both Good Friday and Black Friday, Holy Week and Shark Week. The church calendar does not negate the calendar that separates time into the re-volving cycle of months and days. Instead, it stands as a reminder that something extraordinary occurs in the midst of what seems merely ordinary. The two calendars seem to say conflicting things, but both tell us the truth about ourselves and God's world. If we have God-eyes, we also see that both calendars are also good and beautiful because God is present in and through creation.

6

GOING TO CHURCH WITH BACON-EATERS, DEAD PEOPLE, AND SUPERHEROES

A polar-bear cub asked his mother, "Am I adopted?"

Mother polar bear said, "No, you are our biological offspring, but we would not love you less if you were adopted."

A few days later, the cub asked both parents, "Am I adopted?"

This time they brought out family photos of a pregnant momma bear and his first baby-cub pictures.

A week later, the cub asked once more, "Are you sure I'm not adopted?"

Father bear was getting a bit impatient and said, "We've promised that you weren't adopted and have shown you pictures. Why do you keep pestering us with this adoption stuff?"

The cub replied, "Because I'm just stinkin' cold all the time."

I love adoption as a metaphor for salvation, not least because both of our children are adoptees. Our adoptions created an unusual reality in which two people who have no genetic link to my wife and me live at our house, eat our food, are heirs in our will, and call us mom and dad. Indeed, it is also *their* house and *their* food, and we are *their* parents. We cannot imagine it being otherwise. However, two realities exist together: they have biological parents and adoptive parents. Something new happens at adoption, but the old doesn't cease to exist.

I, too, am an adoptee. Like all Christians, I gained the status of God's child by adoption (Rom 8:15; Gal 3:26). Like all adoptions, this conditions but doesn't change my status as a member of a biological family. I have dual addresses as a citizen of heaven (Phil 3:20) with an H-1B visa that calls me to mission on planet Earth. I am an heir of God's kingdom who gets overdraft notices from my bank. Adoption gave me a new identity, but I still have the same name and picture on my driver's license, the same tendency to salt everything on my plate before I taste it, and even though many Christian athletes like to give God credit for their success, being God's kid hasn't made a dent in my golf handicap. Here it is again: I live in two different worlds with two different families and identities, and it is inevitable that I will encounter incongruity in this. I am confident that I am a polar bear, but it's a bit confusing why I'm also stinkin' cold much of the time.

The incongruities caused by our spiritual adoption are multiplied by the fact that we don't just get a new parent. We get a new family, a really big one with a genealogy that goes all the way back to Adam and Eve. It is crazy enough trying to balance out obligations to your biological kin and your in-laws at Christmas, but when your other family happens to be God's family, we should probably suspect that we will encounter both tension and hilarity. We know that even in families bonded by deep love, our kinfolk drive us crazy and cause us pain at times. It's no different in God's family. Our task in this chapter is to do some ecclesiology—the doctrine of the church—and see if we can better understand what God has in mind for his family.

TEARING DOWN THE WALLS

A French tourist lands in Atlanta and wants to get a taxi to his hotel, but he speaks no English. So when he runs into Bubba and Bubba Junior, he asks, "Parlez-vous français?" and gets only blank stares. "Parla italiano?"

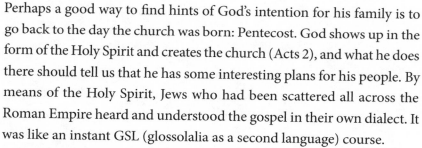

Only shrugs.

"Habla español?"

Same thing. The guy even tries Portuguese and Latin, with no luck.

Finally the tourist just walks away in frustration.

Bubba Junior says, "Wow, Dad, that was amazing! Maybe we ought to learn another language."

His dad responds, "That guy knew five. Lotta good it did him."

Perhaps a good way to find hints of God's intention for his family is to go back to the day the church was born: Pentecost. God shows up in the form of the Holy Spirit and creates the church (Acts 2), and what he does there should tell us that he has some interesting plans for his people. By means of the Holy Spirit, Jews who had been scattered all across the Roman Empire heard and understood the gospel in their own dialect. It was like an instant GSL (glossolalia as a second language) course.

Pentecost was Babel played in reverse. At Babel, nations were divided by language, and they couldn't understand each other (Gen 11:1-9). Now, divided nations who couldn't understand each other could hear the gospel and understand. Before his ascension, Jesus hinted that something big was going to happen: "You will receive power when the Holy Spirit has come upon you; and you will be my witnesses in Jerusalem, in all Judea and Samaria, and to the ends of the earth" (Acts 1:8). However, they probably did not expect fire, Babel's reversal, and the way God would move his church to the ends of the earth. The social fragmentation of Babel was going to be flipped on its head in a way no one anticipated.

A reporter heard that an elderly Jewish man had prayed at the Wailing Wall every day for sixty years. She thought this would be an interesting story, so she went to the wall and found him.

"What do you pray for?" she asked.

> He replied, "I pray that the Jews, the Muslims, and the Christians will someday live in peace and our children can grow up together in safety."
>
> The reporter followed up, "After sixty years, how do you feel about this?"
>
> The old man said, "Like I'm talking to a wall."

It doesn't stop with the Holy Spirit adding Diaspora Jews to the club. In a vision, Peter is told by God to breach an ancient and sacred wall by killing and eating unclean animals (Acts 10:9-16). This taboo was deeply ingrained in Peter, and he strongly resists this command at first, but God is persistent. After three repetitions of this vision and the heavenly voice's insistence that "What God has made clean, you must not call profane" (Acts 10:15), it should not surprise us that Peter was "greatly puzzled" (Acts 10:17). It had to be puzzling when God tells you to eat something that God earlier told you not to eat. Leviticus 11 has a pretty extensive and unambiguous list of what God's people can and can't consume, after all.

By the time he goes to the house of Cornelius, a Gentile, Peter has drawn the right conclusion: if no food is unclean, then no one who eats that food is unclean. After Peter's sermon to those assembled at Cornelius's house, the Gentile world had its own Pentecost. The Holy Spirit came upon them and they spoke in tongues (Acts 10:45-46). It had to be a very difficult thing for Peter and the rest of the early church to wrap their brains around the idea that God's kingdom included bacon-eaters. But if God gives his most precious gift, the Holy Spirit, to Gentiles, it is probably a good idea to baptize them and welcome them to their new family. As Paul puts it, "For he [Christ] is our peace; in his flesh he has made both groups [Jew and Gentile] into one and has broken down the dividing wall, that is, the hostility between us" (Eph 2:14). Peace comes in Christ, and there is no longer any wall to talk to. Besides, bacon makes everything better.

> A couple of old gents, Bud and Gus, were sitting on a park bench when a young couple nearby starting kissing. Bud said, "I can't believe what kids do in public these days. I didn't kiss my wife until our wedding day. Did you?"
>
> Gus said, "Don't know for sure. What was her maiden name?"

Here's what we know so far about God's club. He doesn't seem too choosy about who gets membership in this reformulated version of the chosen people. However, God's plan wasn't just that all sorts of folks would be included in his church. He expects them to become a community of kissers. Five times in the epistles, Jesus' followers were told to greet one other with a holy kiss (Rom 16:16; 1 Cor 16:20; 2 Cor 13:12; 1 Thess 5:26; 1 Pet 5:14). On the surface, this doesn't seem radical since kissing was a common form of greeting in Middle Eastern culture. However, outside of Christianity, folks were selective about who they smooched. Cross-class kissing was taboo in Roman and Jewish settings. But Christianity plowed right over this no-no; slaves and slave owners participated together in this ritual.[1] Outside the church, Jews and Gentiles wouldn't even come into physical contact with each other,[2] let alone kiss, but this wasn't true for Christians. Gender wasn't even a barrier. Women and men kissed in God's community. No wimpy air kiss for these early believers either. The holy kiss was planted on the lips, although Clement of Alexandria directs that it must be "chaste and closed mouth."[3]

There is something going on here that is much more profound than laying a foundation for a lame Christian pickup line (*"Hey, good lookin'.*

---

[1] Although the earliest explicit reference to this comes from circa 202 CE, when Perpetua kisses Felicitas, her slave, prior to both being martyred, we do not find prohibitions against the kissing of slaves in early Christian literature as we do in non-Christian sources. Michael Philip Penn, *Kissing Christians: Ritual and Community in the Late Ancient Church* (Philadelphia: University of Pennsylvania Press, 2005), 33.

[2] It has to be very odd for Peter to say to Cornelius and all his Gentile friends and family gathered at the house, "You yourselves know that it is unlawful for a Jew to associate with or to visit a Gentile" (Acts 10:28).

[3] Clement of Alexandria, *The Instructor*, 3.11, trans. William Wilson, in *Ante-Nicene Fathers*, vol. 2, ed. Alexander Roberts, James Donaldson, and A. Cleveland Coxe (Buffalo, NY: Christian Literature, 1885), www.newadvent.org/fathers/02093.htm.

Holy kiss. It's in the Bible"). Instead, the holy kiss is just one more way God upends the social structures of the day and gives concrete confirmation to Paul's statement that "there is no longer Jew or Greek, there is no longer slave or free, there is no longer male and female; for all of you are one in Christ Jesus" (Gal 3:28). More walls come crashing down.

AND EVEN MORE WALLS COME DOWN

> Listen, I tell you a mystery: We will not all sleep, but we will all be changed. (1 Cor 15:51 NIV)
>
> **SIGN ABOVE THE ENTRANCE TO A CHURCH NURSERY**

> I used to hate going to weddings because all the older people would come up to me, poke me, and say, "You're next."
>
> I finally got them to stop by doing the same thing to them at funerals.

Most of the groups with which we voluntarily associate are not very age-inclusive, so the church is rather unique in this sense. God's people are found all across the human lifespan—diapers (which "will all be changed") to death. Much of our humor centers on the different phases of life and their unique features and challenges (*I've reached the age where rolling a joint now refers to twisting an ankle*). Likewise, many of our jokes deal with the transitions of life—birth (*I felt like a man trapped in a woman's body. Then I was born*),[4] adolescence (*when one is well informed about any subject one doesn't have to study*), marriage (*Shortest sentence possible: "I am." Longest sentence possible: "I do"*), parenthood (*feeding the mouth that bites you*), and death (*the universal cure for life*).

Humor teams up with God's agenda for his people when the church recognizes the spiritual significance of these transitions. So our biological

---

[4]Chris Bliss is the source of this line.

families and friends are folded into the larger body of God's family and friends, and in baptism or infant dedication, confirmation, marriage, and funerals we recognize a bigger reality. These seams in life are not simply financial, social, psychological, and legal realities, although they are these. The church's involvement with hatching, matching, and dispatching indicates that these moments teem with spiritual significance.

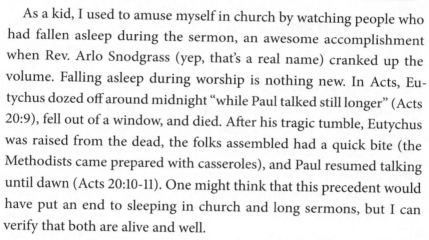

Medium-sized church building for sale. Sleeps four hundred.

As a kid, I used to amuse myself in church by watching people who had fallen asleep during the sermon, an awesome accomplishment when Rev. Arlo Snodgrass (yep, that's a real name) cranked up the volume. Falling asleep during worship is nothing new. In Acts, Eutychus dozed off around midnight "while Paul talked still longer" (Acts 20:9), fell out of a window, and died. After his tragic tumble, Eutychus was raised from the dead, the folks assembled had a quick bite (the Methodists came prepared with casseroles), and Paul resumed talking until dawn (Acts 20:10-11). One might think that this precedent would have put an end to sleeping in church and long sermons, but I can verify that both are alive and well.

My childhood denomination, the Disciples of Christ, was non-creedal. Thus, most of us thought the Apostles' Creed was Carl Weathers's character in the first four *Rocky* movies. Regardless, nothing in the creed was contrary to Reverend Snodgrass's beliefs, including the affirmation of "the communion of saints," the belief that we have ongoing fellowship with everyone in God's family, living and dead. Thus, when we worship, we "come to Mount Zion and to the city of the living God, the heavenly Jerusalem, and to innumerable angels in festal gathering, and to the assembly of the firstborn who are enrolled in heaven, and to God the judge of all, and to the spirits of the righteous made perfect" (Heb 12:22-23). While we share pews with folks who have fallen asleep in a literal sense, we also worship with those who have "fallen asleep" in the biblical sense, as in, died (Dan 12:2; 1 Thess 4:13-14). I still entertain myself by watching people sleep during church, but I've added a new twist. I remind myself that I also am communing with saints from every age and culture who have passed to eternal life by imagining people in my congregation in clothing from different places and periods. Bob looks dashing in his toga.

> I sent the club a wire stating, "PLEASE ACCEPT MY RESIG-
> NATION. I DON'T WANT TO BELONG TO ANY CLUB THAT
> WILL ACCEPT PEOPLE LIKE ME AS A MEMBER."
>
> GROUCHO MARX[5]

From what we have seen so far, it looks like God's sense of humor is once again on display. His club is, after all, the most prestigious club one can imagine. Prestige, under "normal" circumstances, means exclusivity and rigorous candidate screening. Admitting the wrong people damages your group's cool factor. God has a new normal though, one in which there are no wrong people. The gender boundaries that so often exclude? Gone. The racial, cultural, economic, and language differences that tell us who's in and who's out? The wrecking ball took out those walls almost from the very beginning. Your age doesn't make any difference either. God's family includes both ends of the age spectrum and everything in between. Indeed, you don't even need a pulse. When we gather to worship, the living join with the dead in Christ (not intended here as a reference to Presbyterians) before God's throne. Our ironic God offers eternal membership in his club to absolutely everyone.

So if you want to be part of God's family, what are the requirements for adoption? I see two. First, we have to affirm that God and God alone

---

[5]Marx reports sending this telegram to the Friars' Club in Beverly Hills, in Groucho Marx, *Groucho and Me*, 4th ed. (Boston: De Capo Press, 1995), 320.

has the right to be the head of this family, and second, we need to affirm that we have no right to be in the family. So Groucho got it partly right. We don't come close to meeting the membership standards for a club that offers personal access to God and eternal life. God seems to want us there anyway.

GOOD NEWS/BAD NEWS

 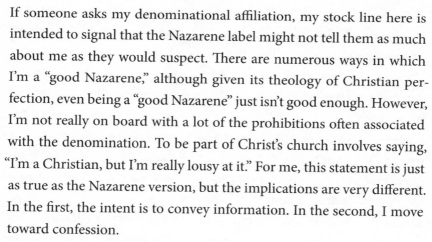

I'm Nazarene, but I'm really lousy at it.

If someone asks my denominational affiliation, my stock line here is intended to signal that the Nazarene label might not tell them as much about me as they would suspect. There are numerous ways in which I'm a "good Nazarene," although given its theology of Christian perfection, even being a "good Nazarene" just isn't good enough. However, I'm not really on board with a lot of the prohibitions often associated with the denomination. To be part of Christ's church involves saying, "I'm a Christian, but I'm really lousy at it." For me, this statement is just as true as the Nazarene version, but the implications are very different. In the first, the intent is to convey information. In the second, I move toward confession.

By stating, "I'm a Christian," I confess that, by faith, I have been saved by Christ. This is the good news of Christianity. Like the teenager who called her dad and said, *The good news is that every smoke alarm in the house works perfectly,* I would prefer to leave it at that. *Gospel* means good news, right? However, just as the "good news" about the smoke alarms is only half the story, our second confession—"but I'm really lousy at it"—cannot be separated from the first. If I am to be saved to Christ, I'll have to admit that I didn't earn it. In short, our confession as Christians parallels one of the most familiar of joke forms, the good news/bad news joke, but with a decisive difference.

> The owner of an art gallery called an artist and said, "I've got some good news and some bad news. The good news is that someone came into the gallery today and asked if I thought the value of your paintings would go up after you were dead. I told him I was quite sure that would be the case. He bought every one of them."
>
> The artist said, "That's amazing. So what's the bad news?"
>
> The gallery owner told him, "The person who bought them was your doctor."

Reversal is a common feature of humor, and it is prominently featured in good news/bad news jokes. The artist believes his fortunes have changed and his art is selling, but the good news is negated by the implication that he won't be around much longer to enjoy it. One scenario destroys the other when they collide. However, in the Christian version of good news/bad news jokes, the two continue in juxtaposition. I don't cease to be saved, nor do I ever get over being a sinner. Don't get me wrong, I'm a good enough Nazarene to believe that the range and frequency of sinful thoughts and actions can and should be reduced with God's help. Indeed, many of us have witnessed amazing redemption stories in which people's lives have been radically transformed. But that's different from saying that we stop being sinners. Once again, we have to deal with what seems to be a massive incongruity. How can we be simultaneously saved and sinner? How can good news coexist with bad news? Moreover, we don't just experience this juxtaposition on the individual level. We feel it in our corporate life together.

A SMELLY ARK

> As has been said, the church is like Noah's ark: The stench inside would be unbearable if it weren't for the storm outside.
>
> **CHARLES COLSON[6]**

---

[6]Charles W. Colson, *Being the Body* (Nashville: W Publishing Group, 2003), 49.

When the kids are doing well, they're my kids. If they mess up, they're my wife's kids. We see the same sort of parental banter after the infamous golden-calf fiasco. No sooner had Moses left for the mountain to receive the Ten Commandments than the grumpy Israelites asked Aaron for a new god (Ex 32:1). Instead of resisting, Aaron gives in immediately. He collected all their gold jewelry, melted it down, made a baby-cow idol, built an altar, and announced a festival of worship for the idol (Ex 32:2-6). When Moses returns, neither he nor God is happy about this. In a darkly funny custody battle in which neither wants to claim the kids, God says to Moses, "Go down, because *your* people, whom *you* have brought up out of Egypt, have become corrupt" (Ex 32:7 NIV, emphasis added). However, Moses isn't taking ownership here, and he responds, "LORD, why should your anger burn against *your* people, whom *you* brought out of Egypt with great power and a mighty hand" (Ex 32:11 NIV, emphasis added)? It isn't any different today. Often, the stench inside the church is so intense that I don't want to be associated with it, and I wonder if God sometimes feels the same way.

This shouldn't surprise us. The church is, first, a collection of flawed, idiosyncratic, and fallen people that, second, is gathered into an institutional structure that, third, addresses the deepest and most life-altering questions of human existence. The combination of any of these two ingredients is highly combustible, and the three together are downright nuclear. Within our churches, we see amazing instances of redemption and restoration, people giving themselves in sacrificial acts of service, folks comforting each other through life-shaking tragedy, and people dedicating their time and skills to model Jesus' love to the children in their congregation. At the same time, we also see shouting matches over the carpet color for the sanctuary remodel, petty spats about music styles, and heresy accusations over obscure points of theology. And these are the same people.

It would be nice if these conflicts remained at a level equivalent to a bunch of twelve-year-olds giving each other wedgies, but sinfulness within the church has claimed far too many victims. On most occasions when a person's faith has been killed or seriously wounded, there is no need to notify the next of spiritual kin. They are quite likely to be the ones who committed the crime. The odd thing is that we should already know that the church will be simultaneously a haven of redemption and a circular firing squad. After all, any worship service worthy of its name includes both praise that God's ark saves us from the deadly storm outside as well as our confession that things inside reek so badly that there's not enough incense to cut through the stench.

CONFESSING

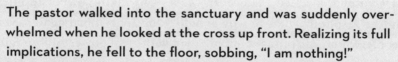

The pastor walked into the sanctuary and was suddenly overwhelmed when he looked at the cross up front. Realizing its full implications, he fell to the floor, sobbing, "I am nothing!"

The head elder came in shortly thereafter, saw the pastor on the floor, and she too fell down and started saying repeatedly, "I'm nothing, O Lord!"

Hearing all the racket from the next room, the janitor saw the two on the floor and was also overcome, fell prostrate, and wailed, "I am nothing!"

The pastor nudged the head elder, pointed to the janitor, and said, "Now, look at who thinks he's nothing!"

We don't go to a comedy club to see heroes. If we want superheroes, the movies offer an abundant supply (more about superheroes later). Instead, we go to comedy clubs to see ourselves, albeit funnier and often exaggerated versions of ourselves. This is why so much of standup, with only a short time to connect with an audience, engages in confession. Jack Benny made a living off of his image for cheapness (*"Any man [referring to Abraham Lincoln] who would walk five miles through the snow, barefoot, just to return a library book so he could save three cents—that's my kind of guy"*); Richard Lewis played the neurotic (*"Sobriety worked for me, but I have so much clarity now I hate myself even more"*); and John Pinette made overeating the center of his routines ("*I can say, 'Feed me, I'm hungry,' in twenty-seven languages"*). Comedic confessions give us a sense of kinship with the person onstage because they are mirrors that allow us to see ourselves.

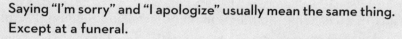

> Saying "I'm sorry" and "I apologize" usually mean the same thing. Except at a funeral.
>
> **DEMETRI MARTIN**

Humor is contextual, so the confessions of a standup routine may not be relevant for understanding Christian confession. For Christians, our shortcomings are not just part of a shtick or stage persona. They are the sins that harm ourselves and others and sadden God. But I think some comparison is worthwhile on a couple of counts.

First, we can't even get to point where we recognize the need to confess without one of humor's tools. Laughter has its roots in the incongruity between what is and what should be, and this ability is at the heart of moral and spiritual discernment. To get a laugh from a one-liner about stinginess, for example, we contrast it with the ideal of generosity, recognize the incongruity, and pass judgment on ourselves. Thus, as Reinhold Niebuhr puts it, "Humour is, in fact, a prelude to faith, and laughter is the beginning of prayer."[7]

While Niebuhr allows that humor affords us the opportunity to identify the chasm between our actual behavior and our ideal, he finds no theological purpose beyond this. In fact, he views humor in confession as a means of obscuring or downplaying our spiritual shortcomings. However, a humorous perspective doesn't just reveal the difference between what we are and what we should be. It also reveals the sheer stupidity of sin, which is on full display a little later in the golden-calf story mentioned a couple of pages ago.

---

[7]Reinhold Niebuhr, "Humour and Faith," in *Discerning the Signs of the Times* (New York: Charles Scribner's Sons, 1946), 111.

After God and Moses finish arguing about whose people the Israelites are, Moses turns his attention to Aaron and is not at all happy with his complicity in the Israelites' idolatry. What is Aaron's response? To paraphrase, he says, "Look, they made me take their gold swag, so I threw it into the fire and, lo and behold, out popped this golden calf" (Ex. 32:24). Are you going to tell me that we shouldn't laugh at the stupidity of exchanging God for a lump of metal and the pitiful "explanation" for why Aaron did it? Of course, the stupidity of sin goes right back to the first one, which results in Adam and Eve attempting to hide from God (Gen 3:8). It is nothing short of ludicrous, and our laughter indicates that we see the absurdity clearly. Since confession is letting God know that we know what God already knows about us, it's silly to think we can hide. We should grieve when we recognize the wreckage caused by our sin, but we should laugh at ourselves as well because that tells us another important truth: sin is just stupid, and attempts at cover-up are even dumber. If grief is present in our humor, our laughter is a healthy form of judgment on ourselves, individually and corporately.

> Guide to Religious Differences:
> Jews don't recognize Jesus as the Messiah.
> Protestants don't recognize the pope as the head of the church.
> Baptists don't recognize each other in a liquor store.

> How many of each does it take to change a light bulb?
> Charismatics: Only one. Hand's already in the air.
> Calvinists: None. Lights will go on and off at predestined times.
> Roman Catholics: None. Candles only.
> Episcopalians: Eight. One to call the electrician, and seven to say how much better they liked the old light bulb.
> Amish: What's a light bulb?

Our spiritual family extends across the globe and across time. However, our expressions of faith occur within specific denominations and congregations. Often our specific group came into existence because of disagreements over doctrine and practice. Tragically, believers have killed each other over such disagreements. We don't do that much anymore, but our Christian tribalism still leads to suspicion and disunity within the Christian family. In addition, it sometimes results in a smugness that assumes that only those who share our beliefs will make it to heaven, and that's only if we don't overshoot it in all of our doctrinal purity.

Self-deprecating humor is disarming because you admit to a vulnerability. This type of humor is important in two ways. First, it indicates that you are confident enough to be able to get over yourself. We transcend ourselves by taking the perspective of others and give a report of what we see. Second, self-deprecating humor communicates to others that you trust them. Healthy families are able to laugh at and with each other because, even though the laughter may reveal real problems, it occurs within a context of love and commitment. The same is true in healthy segments of the church family. Confession of our flaws is an expression of humility and rests on our trust that God forgives.

NO FUN, TOO MUCH DAMN, NOT ENOUGH MENTAL

> How many fundamentalists does it take to screw in a light bulb? That's not funny.

> fun·da·men·tal·ism (fuhn duh **men** tl ˌism)
> Noun.
> 1. No fun, too much damn, not enough mental
> 2. Humorlessness

One of the reasons Jesus' jabs at the pompous Pharisees are so memorable is that this tribe is still around. Today, we know them as fundamentalists. As the first part of the definition says, they are no fun. They have the twenty-pound Bible, a special King James language for prayer, a keen eye for misbehavior, and a long list of heresies that must be crushed whenever they arise. As if all this isn't effective enough as a social repellant, studies show that religious fundamentalists tend to be deficient in humor creation and appreciation.[8] Most of us, after all, prefer to be around people who can laugh and generate laughter when appropriate.

This problem goes deeper than simply boorishness. Fundamentalist humorlessness grows out of an unwillingness to acknowledge incongruity in the world or in oneself. Since a basic incongruity of Christian life is that we exist as both saved and sinner, unwillingness to acknowledge this has serious spiritual implications. Sure, the fundamentalist will engage in confessional prayer, but they also tend to work from their own list of orthodox behaviors and doctrines. When you shoot first and draw the target around the bullet hole, it's easy to hit the bullseye on everything on your list and assume you don't have much to confess. But a lot of other folks are not doing so well when measured against your list, so there's a lot of "damn" in store for them. Still, I admire fundamentalists for one thing: they take Christianity seriously enough that they want to stand out as heroes of the faith. However, their vision of Christian heroism may be a bit off.

CHRISTIAN SUPERHEROES

 Superman is in love with Wonder Woman, but she just wants to be Super Friends with him. It's awkward—super-awkward.

My nomination for greatest T-shirt ever has Jesus sitting in the midst of several quite recognizable superheroes saying, "And that's how I saved the world." Although some attempts have been made to create Christian comic-book superheroes (Captain Salvation, Christian

---

[8]Vassilis Saroglou, "Religiousness, Religious Fundamentalism, and Quest as Predictors of Humor Creation," *International Journal for the Psychology of Religion* 12, no. 3 (July 2002): 177-88.

Knight, Revelators), this genre hasn't done well. Dying on a cross to defeat evil isn't how the Hulk does it. Christianity does have its heroes, to be sure. But since "saved" takes on different meanings in Christianity than it does in superhero movies, Christianity's superheroes turn out to be a bit different as well.

One way to illustrate the differences between our society's superheroes and those of Scripture is to glance at Scripture's best-known superhero list, the so-called "Hall of Faith" in Hebrews 11. These individuals engage in quests so daring that one cannot help but find them heroic. You know the great deeds. Noah builds the ark. David expands the boundaries of Israel. Moses leads the Israelites out of Egypt. Abraham hangs on for decades to the impossible but eventually fulfilled promise of a son. Their heroic feats were supplemented by a supporting cast with equally inspiring acts of faith: "Others were tortured, refusing to accept release, in order to obtain a better resurrection. Others suffered mocking and flogging, and even chains and imprisonment. They were stoned to death, they were sawn in two, they were killed by the sword; they went about in skins of sheep and goats, destitute, persecuted, tormented—of whom the world was not worthy" (Heb 11:35-38). Most of us, if we are honest, must admit that it is unlikely we could sustain this degree of courage. So, as these words state, with a level of profundity that Wayne and Garth could never have imagined, "we're not worthy."

This "Hall of Faith" heroism is real, but God adds his usual twist. The Bible is also brutally honest about these heroes' failures, and they are not mere blemishes. Noah celebrates God's miraculous delivery from a worldwide flood by getting drunk and naked (Gen 9:20-25). David commits adultery with another man's wife, gets her pregnant (2 Sam 11:5), and arranges for the husband's death to cover up the ugly mess (2 Sam 11:14-17). Moses? On the lam for murder (Ex 2:11-15). And the father of faith? We could mention the time when Abraham passes off Sarah as his sister so he could save his own hide (Gen 20:2), or that

Ishmael thing that turned out oh-so-well (Gen 16:1-16), or Abraham laughing when he was informed by divine messengers that he would be a daddy within the year.

> The invisible man had an imaginary girlfriend. He doesn't see her anymore. He said she wasn't being real with him. If there's anything he hates, it's a lack of transparency.

If we are going to understand what it means to be God's people, it helps to see how Christianity redefines heroism. And standing our cultural notion of heroism on its head seems to be one of God's favorite jokes. One common characteristic of Christianity's heroes is that somewhere along the line, they fail, often magnificently. In that way, our heroes look a lot like us. Not so with movie superheroes. Bruce Wayne, as Bruce Wayne, looks pretty normal, even if abnormally handsome, in every comic-book, TV, or movie incarnation of his character. However, Bruce Wayne as Batman looks pretty odd, especially since he wears his underwear over his tights and has a belt holding up his skivvies. He would certainly stick out at Burger King. In fact, every superhero has to stick out in some weird way to be recognized as a superhero. Even the Invisible Man looks strange by not looking like anything at all. By contrast, in the midst of his heroics in his faith journey, Abraham looks exactly like Abraham, except older.

Here's where things get really good, and really odd. In the Christian story, our superheroes are the ones who get saved. Indeed, the definition of heroism in Christianity seems to be an admission of need and reliance on a savior. Ironically, our Savior, the only one who has any real superpower, dies in the process of saving us. This goes beyond a redefinition of salvation and heroism because it makes superheroes of all who throw themselves on God's mercy. We stand in awe of the superheroes of American culture. However, we stand as equals with God's superheroes. We get saved in the same way they do.

THE INSIDE JOKE

> I used to think that the urethra and the testes were the same thing. Then I realized there was a vas deferens between them.

> A goy is a person who, if observed at or before time *t* is a girl but if observed after time *t* is a boy.

The first joke slays at a urology conference, and the second one should elicit a smile from a Jewish physicist, but both would leave many people confused about the humor in these quips. Humor requires shared knowledge, so unless you know that the vas deferens is a duct between the urethra and the testes, the wordplay on similar sounding phrases will be lost on you. In this sense, all humor is inside humor. In the narrower sense of the term, inside jokes remind us of our identity and what makes us unique. Thus, the inside jokes and family stories at a urology conference will be markedly different from those that pop up at Comic Con.

> Mr. Johnson went in for his annual examination, and when it was over, the doctor re-entered the examination room with a grim expression. "Mr. Johnson, you need to sit down. I've got a couple of bits of bad news for you."
>
> After Mr. Johnson sat down, the doctor said, "I'm afraid you have colon cancer, and it's well advanced."
>
> Mr. Johnson replied, "Okay. Not good. What's the other bad news?"
>
> "Well," said the doctor, "you also have Alzheimer's disease."
>
> Mr. Johnson said, "Thank goodness. I thought you were going to tell me I had cancer."

This joke sums up my family medical history. Both of my parents had colon cancer, and my mom had Alzheimer's. (*Thanks mom. I'll never forget you. But if I do, it's your fault.*) This medical history finds its way into our family's inside jokes about feeding marshmallows to dogs,

145

which mom did in her advanced stage of dementia. We don't laugh because Alzheimer's is funny. Instead, our inside jokes and family stories remind us of the journeys we have taken together. They connect us to our history and to each other by reminding us of who we are. And since laughter is a means of showing approval, these jokes and stories are a conduit for expressing love.

> Right now I'm having amnesia and déjà vu at the same time. I think I've forgotten this before.
>
> **STEVEN WRIGHT**

> After forty years of wandering in the wilderness, the Israelites finally reached the Promised Land. They were overjoyed that they could finally sleep indoors away from bugs, snakes, and predators, and had a convenient place to cook their food and use the bathroom.
> Then someone said, "Hey, anyone want to go camping?"

Seen from one perspective, this book is about Christianity's inside humor. God became a human. Outsiders don't think that's funny. To them, it seems like a naked contradiction. However, without this, Christianity doesn't exist. Another joke is that we are both animals and spiritual beings, and this results in our funny life. The inside joke in this chapter is that we are simultaneously saved and sinner, and whenever we meet in worship, we tell ourselves this so we don't forget that we are both, as strange as it seems.

Alzheimer's isn't part of my Christian family's history, but amnesia most definitely is. This amnesia has a sinister result, because we don't just forget where we put our keys or why we went into the pantry. We forget God, and, *déjà vu*, we do it again and again. What makes this amnesia so confounding is that God knows our tendencies toward forgetfulness and gives us all sorts of prompts. Unleavened bread should remind God's people of how they were freed from slavery (Deut 16:1-4). God's commands are mnemonic devises to prompt our memory about whom we belong to (Ps 78:5-7). Rainbows should evoke thoughts of God's covenant (Gen 9:12-17), and tassels on clothing (Num 15:38-40) should spark awareness of our unique family connections. When the Israelites crossed into the Promised Land, twelve stones were set up to remind them of how God brought them out of Egypt and preserved them through forty years of camping (Josh 4:19-24). My rural upbringing taught me that if you find a turtle on top of a fence post, you can be certain it didn't get there by itself. Likewise, you know that twelve stones don't just appear on the banks of the Jordan, and one of the family stories should have immediately sprung to mind. If none of this works, circumcision (Gen. 17:9-13) should surely jog the memory.

Spiritual amnesia must be hereditary, because the apostles have to keep reminding the New Testament church of who God made them to be. They are to be a united people because "there is one body and one Spirit, just as you were called to the one hope of your calling, one Lord, one faith, one baptism, one God and Father of all, who is above all and through all and in all" (Eph 4:4-6). A three-year-old clearly grasps the concept of "one" and knows how to properly apply it, but the early church doesn't seem to get it. So in just one letter, Paul has to deal with divisions over leaders (1 Cor 1:10-17), lawsuits (1 Cor 6:1-8), the Lord's Supper (1 Cor 11:17-34), and the gifts of the Spirit (1 Cor 12-14). Even though the church is fresh and new, the Epistles reveal that these sorts of divisions occur everywhere. We keep forgetting what God has called us to in defragmenting the church, but we continue finding novel ways to separate ourselves from other family members. So one of the inside jokes of the church is dark humor. We often forget that we forget to remember what God has done for us and who we are supposed to be.

DIVINE AMNESIA

> An old golfer was fearful he would have to give up the game because his eyesight was fading, and he couldn't track the ball. However, his neighbor said that he had a friend who didn't golf but loved to walk. Best of all, he had the eyes of an eagle and could spot for the golfer. This was great news, and the two men met at the golf course the next morning.
>
> The golfer hit his first drive but lost sight of it. He turned to his new friend and asked, "Did you see where that one went?"
>
> "Sure did."
>
> "So where is it?"
>
> "I forgot."

The spiritual carnage that has resulted from forgetting God doesn't seem to leave room for laughter. To laugh in the midst of this gives the impression of flippancy toward sinfulness. Again, I want to state that I have no desire to be squishy on sin. Quite the opposite. But I do think there is still room for laughter, because another one of the church's inside jokes is that God himself has a gracious form of amnesia. Jeremiah tells us that God forgets our sin (Jer 31:34; compare Is 43:25). No one who has read Jeremiah will accuse him of being a happy-face prophet. During his life, God's people are bounced from captivity by one nation to another, Jerusalem is sacked and burned, and the temple is destroyed. All this happens, he tells us, because the people have forgotten God (Jer 2:32; 18:15; 23:27). In the midst of all this tragedy, he assures us that God will forget our sin. Our pigheaded and rebellious forgetfulness is trumped by God's loving amnesia. For the moment, exile and destruction are real, but they do not get the last word.

Some of the holiest moments I've observed involve a parent and adult child talking about the latter's youthful hijinks. These conversations often include a lot of laughter punctuated by the phrase, "You really put us through hell during that time." The hell was real, but so is the forgiveness and restoration. We don't laugh about the past simply because the statute of limitations has run out on punishment for misdeeds. Forgiveness is often the precursor of laughter. God forgives and forgets, and in this forgiveness, we experience tiny fragments of resurrection.

A PECULIAR PEOPLE

> My uncle was in a horrible car accident the other night. He wasn't driving at the time, but he was supposed to be.

God created us as social beings, so it shouldn't shock us that the groups and communities to which we belong enrich our lives. However, they do not offer salvation. Only the church does that, and since its aim is unique, we expect that this group will have unique features. Indeed, it does. The equality of the members within this club is not grounded in some political concept of universal human rights, but in the recognition of the universality of human wrongs. Christians belong to a kingdom in which we are invited to call our absolute sovereign "Daddy," the same Lord who had the unspeakable name of YHWH. It is a kingdom whose ruler claims authority over the entire universe, but it has no deeds to any real estate on file. The church may not be a comedy club, but by the standards we usually use to determine who should have a right to club membership, this is a comedic club.

The awkward incongruity of our two worlds is a paradox, but it is not alien to Christ-followers because we experience it at every turn. We know of many things that are not, but they are supposed to be. We know that God's people are supposed to be one body (Rom 12:5; 1 Cor 12:12), but we have ten thousand denominational names that prove that we are not. We join with the angels in praising God, but usually a halftone flat. And we refuse to sing with angels or anyone else if we don't like the style of music. The heroes of our faith are simultaneously martyrs and murderers. God knocks out all the walls that separate us by race, economic status, and gender, and we keep rebuilding them. The fact that we carry the treasure of salvation in earthen vessels (2 Cor 4:7) reads like a punch line. If nothing else, it seems like lousy packaging. Still, we experience the paradox of being both saved and sinner at every turn. Perhaps the King James translation of 1 Peter 2:9 gets it right when it describes us as "a peculiar people."

We should still weep about the fact that we are sinners, but it shouldn't drown out our laughter. The church's laughter at sin and all its ugly consequences is not denial or escapism. It is instead a theological statement. It is an expression of confidence that despite the pain of sin, God does heal and will heal decisively and finally. Laughter is our confession that Jesus is Lord, a lordship we grasp clearly only when we know Jesus as the gracious one who separates our sin from us "as far as the east is from the west" (Ps 103:12). Jesus is, after all, the means by which God forgets sin. Holy laughter, then, is an affirmation that the only thing stronger than our bondage to sin is God's faithfulness to us. The bad news is really, really bad. The good news, however, is even better than sin's badness.

INTERLUDE TWO

ESTHER AS COMEDY

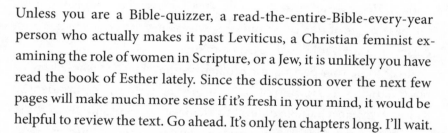

What if God is a comedian doing his act in front of an audience that's afraid to laugh?

VOLTAIRE

Unless you are a Bible-quizzer, a read-the-entire-Bible-every-year person who actually makes it past Leviticus, a Christian feminist examining the role of women in Scripture, or a Jew, it is unlikely you have read the book of Esther lately. Since the discussion over the next few pages will make much more sense if it's fresh in your mind, it would be helpful to review the text. Go ahead. It's only ten chapters long. I'll wait.

Back now? As you read through it, a question that has puzzled Christians through the ages might have popped into your head: Why is the book of Esther even in the Bible? God isn't mentioned at all, and the only things that sound religious are a single reference to fasting (Esther 4:15-16) and the "for just such a time as this" quote that may imply that God's providence is at work (Esther 4:14). In fact, except for chapter nine, when the Jews gain favored status and celebrate with a bloody vengeance on their opponents (no, it wasn't banishment to the island of perpetual tickling, as in the VeggieTales version), nothing in the book would get it banned from a public school. In general, though, Esther doesn't read like the Bible-y stuff Christians expect to see in God's Word. Because of this, John Calvin, who uses Bible references in his writings as liberally as Texans use catsup, refers to Esther only once. Luther goes further. He doesn't just ignore it but instead says, "I am so great an enemy to the second book of the Maccabees, and to Esther, that I wish they had not come to us at all, for they have too many heathen unnaturalities."[1]

Let's contrast the Christian why-is-Esther-in-the-Bible question with the Jewish attitude toward the book. Esther is the foundation of Purim, one of Judaism's five annual feasts. Rather than ignoring Esther, the entire book is read aloud twice each year, once the night of Purim and again the next morning. Moreover, it is read in a way that makes it quite memorable, as we will see. Ironically, then, the average Jewish layperson is probably as familiar with the book of Esther as with any book in Hebrew Scripture. So while Christians tend to stuff Esther into the basements of our consciousness, why is it front and center for Judaism, and what might we learn from them about this book?

It could be that part of our problem is that we don't know how to read Esther. A basic rule of biblical interpretation is genre identification. We read a parable differently than we read a psalm. Proverbs is not interpreted in the same way as Revelation, otherwise we read wrongly. However, one problem is that we aren't always certain how to identify genres that don't have obvious parallels to contemporary literary styles. So how should we read Esther? Because the book is set in a real historical situation—Jewish subjugation in the Persian Empire—and we have an undisputed historical figure—Ahasuerus (or Xerxes)—as a key figure in the account, it is often read as historical narrative. However, if we read Esther as a historical account that doesn't factor God into the events, it isn't clear why we should regard it as holy and authoritative. But what if the book of Esther is more like comedy? What if God tells us things we desperately need to remember and does so in joke form? What if our hesitation about Esther arises because we are an audience afraid to laugh at God's humor?

---

[1]Martin Luther, *The Table Talk of Martin Luther* (Philadelphia: Lutheran Publication Society, 2004), 27.

COMEDIC ELEMENTS IN ESTHER

> Insomnia: Doing what you are supposed to do two-thirds of the day at the wrong time.

Why should we read Esther as comedy? One quick answer is that, in its broadest definition, a comedy is a story with a joyful conclusion. Esther certainly has a happy ending, unless you are Haman, one of his ten sons, or one of their seventy-five thousand fellow Agagites who are done in at the end of the book. However, there are also reasons within the text of Esther itself and in the Jewish celebration of Purim (thus, the Jewish interpretation of Esther) that support a humorous hermeneutic.

First, the story is just a tad too tidy for historical narrative. Mordecai "just happens" to overhear the assassination plot (Esther 2:21-23) and rather offhandedly encourages Esther to conceal her Jewish identity (Esther 2:10). Haman "just happens" to hear Ahasuerus refer to the great honors to be bestowed on the nation's benefactor and assumes he will be the honoree (Esther 6:6-9). Esther "just happens" to win the beauty contest (Esther 2:12-18). And speaking of unlikely plot features, why is Mordecai's Jewish identity known, but his cousin Esther's is not?

The timing of the various plot elements is very "convenient." There is never a good time to have insomnia if you are trying to sleep, but it afflicts Ahasuerus at just the right time (Esther 6:1) to lead the story toward its conclusion. Reading from the annals is perhaps the perfect cure for insomnia, but the king doesn't seem to be the sort of person who is very interested in the mundane affairs of state. It all works out well for Mordecai, though, because Ahasuerus is reminded that he "just happened" to forget to acknowledge the person who saved him from assassination (Esther 6:3).

Esther fingers the villain in the nick of time to save her fellow Jews (Esther 7:6). Finally, the whole story line falls apart without a king who is so clueless that Haman's arrogance and evil intentions go right over his head, and he misinterprets the presence of Haman on Esther's couch as an attempted sexual assault (Esther 7:7-8). This all feels too coincidental when compared to the manner in which history usually unfolds. Doesn't it read more like the script for a sitcom? Of course, the devout reader will tell us that God is the unseen director who engineers what only seems to be a series of fortunate coincidences, and that is precisely the point. Part of the joke is that the unnamed God is the star of the show, and the actors, who think they are calling the shots, are actually playing the roles that God has written into his script.

> Lone Ranger: "There are Indians on the left and right. They are in front of us and behind us. What are we going to do, Tonto?"
> Tonto: "What do you mean 'we,' Paleface?"

This old and questionable joke is a reminder that the main characters in Esther are more like stock types than moral exemplars, a common feature in comedy throughout the ages. When Mordecai pleas with Esther to petition the king to save her people, she has a brief "what do you mean *we* Jews?" moment, and Mordecai only gets her cooperation when he reminds her that being the queen will not save her neck when it is discovered that she is Jewish (Esther 4:13). Thus when she decides to make her plea to the king, it isn't clear whether her words, "and if I perish, I perish" (Esther 4:16), indicate courage or resignation. Prior to this point, Esther got to where she was by winning a beauty contest and, until her hand is forced, she does nothing to improve the lot of her people. Thus, she is a hero, but the imperfect hero so often found in comedy.

Ahasuerus has an extensive kingdom with 127 provinces (Esther 1:1). Administering such a far-flung realm would be enough to keep any sovereign busy. Yet Ahasuerus is more interested in throwing a 180-day party followed by a seven-day feast (Esther 1:4-5) than actually, you know, ruling. He is so incurious that he doesn't even know that his new queen is Jewish, nor does he ask any questions when Haman proposes his plan to exterminate the Jews (Esther 3:10-11). His drunk courtiers convince him to depose his previous queen, Vashti, when she refuses to parade before them. The courtiers make the ludicrous claim that this will encourage all wives to disobey their husbands (Esther 1:10-18). His brilliant idea for finding a replacement queen? Hold a Miss Persia beauty pageant, of course.

Haman is the caricature of a villain, the very embodiment of evil and conceit. If you get the sense that you should hiss and boo whenever he shows up, you are on the right track. He arrogantly demands that the other court officials bow before him (Esther 3:2), and when Mordecai refuses to give in to Haman's pretensions, it is not enough to get rid of him. Every Jew must die. When Haman overhears the king's plan to give honors to a great person, he naturally assumes that it is about him. To get revenge on Mordecai, he can't just build the gallows. Instead, he constructs a seventy-five-foot-tall mother-of-all-gallows gallows (Esther 5:14).

Mordecai seems like a nice enough guy who cares for his orphaned cousin. However, he changes her Jewish name, Hadassah, to Esther to conceal her Jewish identity from the king. His big act of heroism results from a chance overhearing of an assassination plot. When the Jews are saved from Haman's wicked schemes, Mordecai's response, after he is made second in command, is as bloody as the ethnic cleansing planned by Haman.

In drama, character development is a major feature. In contrast, the main characters of Esther are two-dimensional types who could be plugged into almost any comedic plot line. Each plays a role in making the story happen as it does, but often unintentionally. Besides the brief "for just such a time as this" reference (Esther 4:14), they say or do little that is designed to spur us toward moral excellence. Instead, comedic

characters remind us of all the people we know: the powerful but buf-
foonish ruler ("everybody likes you, under penalty of death," according
to VeggieTales), the evil Snidely Whiplash, the pretty heroine, and the
nice guy caught up in circumstances beyond his control.

A third indicator that we should read Esther as comedy is that political satire runs throughout the book. The story pokes fun at the
Persian Empire's grotesque excesses. The reader sees that, despite its
outward appearance of invincibility, the empire on the inside is a circus
run by a bumbler who lacks the moral discernment to see that his
number-two man is a conniver and bigot. Everything is supersized,
from the 180-day party with a no-limit, open bar where wine is served
in golden goblets, to the outlandish expectations that Queen Vashti
strut her stuff before the wine-soaked sycophants, to the off-the-charts
beauty treatments required of Esther before she appears before the king
(Esther 2:12), to the extreme demand that the king exterminate all the
Jews, to the ludicrous pomposity of Haman and the seventy-five-foot-
high gallows he erects for the hanging of Mordecai.

Political satire is a sneaky form of humor, which makes it fun for
those in on the joke. When the glory, wealth, and pomp of the Persian
court are described, the oppressors take it as a compliment and recognition of their favored status. In their view, they are indeed powerful and maybe even immortal. At the same time, the subjugated
satirists are snickering at the pompous jerks who are willfully blind
to the suffering of those who are the source of the empire's wealth.
They see Persia's silly pretentiousness, its ineptitude, and its tempo-
rality. The topper on this joke is that this empire, which is ready to
exterminate the Jews at the beginning of the story, becomes the un-
witting vehicle by which God's people receive salvation and their enemies are routed. Persia believes it is in touch with reality and con-
trols its vast kingdom, but the empire doesn't have a clue about what
is really happening.

Hanging the wrong person: Good intentions, poor execution.

Haman's famous last words: "I thought I was getting off a bit too easy for my crime. Turns out I was right. I didn't realize that when the judge said, 'Sentence: temporarily suspended,' he meant that I was to be hanged."

The final comedic element found throughout Esther is one of the most stock devices of the genre: reversal. Of course, the laugh-out-loud reversal is when Mr. Inflated-Ego Haman discovers that the over-the-top rewards for saving the king, a list Haman himself concocts, are to be given instead to his archenemy, Mordecai. To add insult to injury, Haman himself, the king's second in command, gets to be the messenger boy (Esther 6:11). But this is not the only reversal. Hadassah the Jewish orphan girl becomes Esther the Queen of Persia, Haman is hanged from the gallows he built for Mordecai, and those who oppose Esther's people are slaughtered rather than the Jews.

For these reasons and some that will come later, it seems plausible that we should read Esther not just as humor, but as low humor. Instead of clever bon mot, highbrow sarcasm, or the private inside jokes of the learned arts, Esther is farce and caricature with a hint of slapstick.[2] Esther is not the sort of literature designed to appeal to the cultivated and sophisticated wit, but to the raucous, unwashed, and subjugated masses. This is not to say that Esther is historical fiction. However, if we take note only of the historical elements in the book, we never see that God is playing a prank on all who would blot out the existence of his people. The powerless know that what we so often call fate or coincidence is

---

[2]Debbie Blue argues that we ought to read this as farce. See Debbie Blue, "Biblical Farce: The Book of Esther Laughs at Empire," *Christian Century*, January 20, 2016, 32-33. Others argue that it should be understood as burlesque. See Adele Berlin, *The JPS Bible Commentary—Esther* (Philadelphia: Jewish Publication Society, 2001). While elements of farce and burlesque are present alongside political satire, I fear that attempting to specify a particular form of comedy too strictly imposes contemporary categories on an ancient work.

something more for those who have faith. They are in on God's joke—the unnamed player in the entire book is the Holy One who works in and through historical events to bring salvation. To commemorate it, they throw a loud and crazy party annually to celebrate God's gracious joke, because they recognize that God's joke is for them.

PERFORMING ESTHER AS COMEDY

When an entire people has been spared from extermination, a celebratory feast seems to be the appropriate response, and that is what happens once the king reverses Haman's evil plan (Esther 8:17). And the Jews continue to recall this event annually in a rollicking good party called Purim. When they gather on the evening of the fourteenth day of Adar, participants do not listen passively while the book of Esther is read. Instead, they cheer when Mordecai's and Esther's names are heard, and jeer and use obnoxiously loud noisemakers to show their scorn whenever Haman's name occurs (fifty-four times in most translations). Haman's name is written on the bottom of shoes, and celebrants stomp their feet as they hiss and boo to blot out his memory. The reading of Esther is followed by a feast, and participants are expected to drink a lot of wine. I mean *a lot*. The Talmud says that they should consume enough alcohol that eventually they are unable to distinguish between "blessed be Mordecai" and "cursed be Haman."[3] I can't give you exact blood alcohol levels here, but we are without doubt well into designated-driver territory.

Children play a much larger role in Purim than in the other Jewish festivals. They are encouraged to wear costumes as a reminder that God is always present with his people, even when he is unseen and his name is unspoken. During the celebration, plays and skits are performed, usually by the kids. Silly songs abound, and there are sometimes parodies in which a fake rabbi purposely messes up the reading and ritual,

---

[3]Talmud, Megillah, 7b. See http://halakhah.com/pdf/moed/Megilah.pdf.

generating lots of giggles from the youngsters. And of course you get the costumed kids' beauty contest to see who gets to be Queen Esther. The whole celebration is rowdy and loud. Just the way kids like it.

The following morning, there is a big breakfast with another reading of Esther, complete again with boos and cheers. During the day, friends and neighbors exchange gifts of food and drink, usually delivered by children if they are present in the household, and alms are collected for the needy, in accordance with Mordecai's directive for future remembrances of their delivery from extermination (Esther 9:22).

CHRISTIANS AND ESTHER

I have a strong suspicion that Gentile Christianity's perplexity about Esther's inclusion in the Bible arises because we have little experience with being a persecuted people, fearful that our very existence could be blotted out at any moment. This sensitivity, however, is constantly in the minds of our Jewish neighbors. As a result, they know this book. They read Esther, and it fortifies them. The genre may be low comedy, but when your existence as a people is precarious, the message of Esther ranks high on the seriousness index.

For most Western Christians, however, Esther may have an equally relevant but darker message. The perks of Persia, at least for now, are ours. We feel secure, wealthy, and powerful; we enjoy the equivalent of good wine in gold goblets. Thus, it is easy to conclude that we are invincible when we are actually nothing more than numb and stupid. It is difficult to put ourselves in the place of Esther, who, realizing the precarious nature of her situation, can only say, "If I perish, I perish."

Because of our sense of security and well-being, I'm not certain most Western Christians really understand a feast like Purim. When we feast, we do so because we can. Like the Persian court at the beginning of Esther, we feast because it's easy, enjoyable, and well within our budget. But how would Purim take on a new significance if you were hated, marginalized, impoverished, oppressed, or in captivity almost every time the festival rolled around? Purim looks backward toward a time when God miraculously saved them from disaster, and it looks forward to a time when Messiah will come and their salvation will be complete. However, throughout the ages, Jews have almost always celebrated Purim under grim and oppressive circumstances. In these situations, people do not feast because they can, but because they must. If hope is to remain alive, Purim is a necessary reminder that God has acted to save his people and will do so decisively when Messiah comes.

While many Christians view Esther as a book of only minor importance, a quite different judgment is rendered by the great Jewish scholar Maimonides (Rambam). He says, "The holiday of Purim will never be abolished. Even at the end of days when all commemorations of our travails will not apply, the Book of Esther will be like the Five Books of Moses and last for all eternity."[4] Other rabbis have concurred with his evaluation that Purim will be the only one of the five annual festivals that will continue to be celebrated after Messiah comes.[5]

While we have a fundamental disagreement with our Jewish neighbors about whether Jesus is the Messiah, Christians should learn a few things from them about a proper response to Messiah's coming. They can teach us that Jesus' appearance in our world is cause for giddy celebration. Their performance of Esther as a comedy places the book in the proper context. God works behind the scenes through ordinary people and brings salvation in surprising ways. If any group understands tragedy, marginalization, and exile, it is the Jews. But when a faithful God enters history, comedy and celebration become more real and durable than tragedy and mourning. The solemn and tearful plaints of Lamentations are replaced by the noisy and joyful

---

[4]Rambam, *Laws of Megillah*, 2:18, in Roy S. Neuberger, "Why Purim Is Forever," JewishPress.com, February 29, 2012, www.jewishpress.com/indepth/opinions/why-purim-is-forever/2012/02/29/.
[5]Monford Harris, "Purim: The Celebration of Dis-order," *Judaism* 26, no. 2 (Spring 1977): 170.

celebration that followed, and continues to follow, God's great comedic reversals in Esther.

I think Maimonides gets it right; when Messiah comes, it's time to party. In fact, it is inappropriate not to do so. But Christians will need to make a slight adjustment to the celebration. While we believe that Messiah has come, we also believe that Messiah is coming again. So perhaps Christians need a modified Purim for the present, in which we remember joyfully that Messiah's death and resurrection break the power of sin, but we still await a time when the annihilation of sin and death is complete in Christ's return. Then, we can read Esther with new eyes, eyes through which we perceive the now unseen God as a gracious and loving comedian who brings us in on his joke for us and invites us to laugh with him. And perhaps we should view this future when Messiah returns as the eternal Purim celebration, a time when extravagant festivity is now just another day (although we may need to rethink the Talmud's over-the-top alcohol policy for the celebration). It is to this vision of Messiah's second coming that we now turn.

7

DOES THIS ESCHATOLOGY MAKE MY END LOOK BIG?

I do not know if you noticed this, but one day on the liturgical calendar was conspicuously absent from chapter four's discussion of Holy Week: Holy Saturday. It is easy to understand why we fix our attention on the history-altering events of Good Friday and Easter Sunday, but what are we to make of the in-between day? Holy Saturday is right there on the liturgical calendar, but no Saturday events are recorded in Scripture's narratives. So what is the point of giving a significant-sounding name to a day on which nothing happened?

I have come to conclude that the Bible actually has plenty to say about Holy Saturday. Our lives as Christ-followers is situated between Good Friday's gloom and Easter's new life. Thus, Holy Saturday is a metaphor for the paradoxical tug of two opposing realities that bookend this day. We still experience the death and rot of Friday, but Scripture also reminds us that we participate in the resurrection life that comes with Easter Sunday. Holy Saturday's "in-betweenness" is a reminder for another one of Christianity's apparent incongruities. Our life is simultaneously Friday and Sunday. With Sunday, God's conquest of evil and death is present and real; but in our Friday, this consummation is not yet. So we live in the tension between the already and the not yet, two mutually opposed realities that seem incapable of coexistence.

> OK, maybe I can't spell Armageddon. It's not like it's the end of the world.

This chapter looks forward to Sunday's "not yet," the future final redemption God has planned for his fallen creation. In other words, we are going to talk about what theologians call "eschatology," the study of the "last things." We all are fascinated by the future and its unknowns, and Christians since the beginning of our faith have scoured the Bible looking for clues about how and when God will bring an end to evil. So my job in this chapter will be to provide a definitive timeline of end-time events, name the participants in the battle of Armageddon (ran that through spell check just to be sure), and reveal the true identity of Gog and Magog. Just kidding.

I don't plan to address a number of topics many Christians expect to see in a chapter on eschatology, and for two simple reasons. First, history provides numerous examples of people whose extensive study of Scripture resulted in finely tuned timetables and flow charts for the end of the world. Most have been spectacularly wrong, while the jury is still out on other predictions.[1] Since smart people have failed at this task, it seems wise that I, a philosopher with little training in biblical studies, avoid definitive claims about the obscure passages of Daniel and Revelation. Second, we need to remember that those who were most certain about the details of the Messiah's first coming missed the whole thing. God caught everyone off-guard, and it is safe to believe that God hasn't run out of surprises yet for the Messiah's second coming. So I'll heed Reinhold Niebuhr's cautionary advice on eschatological details: "It is unwise for Christians to claim any knowledge of either the furniture of heaven or the temperature of hell."[2] However, the subject is eschatology,

---

[1] For a survey of end-times predictions across the history of the church, see Richard Kyle, *The Last Days Are Here Again* (Grand Rapids: Baker, 1998).
[2] Reinhold Niebuhr, *The Nature and Destiny of Man: A Christian Interpretation* (New York: Charles Scribner's Sons, 1943), 2:294.

which almost demands a little conjecture about the future, so I will engage in a bit of speculative eschatology at the end of the chapter.

Even though many eschatological topics will be ignored, certain things about God's promised future are knowable with faithful certainty, and we will focus on these. For example, we know that all tyrannies—political, spiritual, physical, economic, or otherwise—are defeated in the end. In addition, we know that God will be "all in all" (1 Cor 15:28), which results in the drying of all tears and the death of all death (Rev 21:4). Finally, we know that the wheels are already in motion for the consummation. All of this seems a lot more central to Christian faith than narrowing down the identity of the Beast (although the Bible is clear that the proper baking temperature for roast beast is 666 degrees). It's a big enough end for me.

GOD'S DEPARTMENT OF WEIGHTS AND MEASURES

> The sign said, "Seating is limited." I think that was supposed to make me feel nervous, but I'm actually happy about it because I like to sit in the back row. If there were an unlimited number of chairs, it would be logically impossible to have a back-row seat, so I wouldn't like where I would have to sit.

We don't often think about how much of life is governed by things that can be measured, weighed, and timed. That's because time, space, and the nature of the objects around us are givens; they are the deterministic structures and rules within which life operates. Regardless of who you are, time is the great equalizer. All human life moves at the rate of exactly sixty minutes per hour. We are spatially limited and cannot be in Boston and Bangor at the same time, gravity does what it does, and even though it's inconvenient, your suitcase is the size that it is and it either will or it will not fit into the overhead bin. So if there's a statement as obvious as "space is limited," it has to be the phrase "time is limited."

That's the nature of spaces and times. They are quantifiable and finite, and they stand as constant reminders that we too are limited and mortal.

> "Time flies," we're told. I'm okay with that, but I think it's unfair that it doesn't have to go through the TSA checkpoint and always ends up in first-class. And if time does fly, why is my plane always late?

The tyrannical nature of time has been recognized since antiquity, as evidenced by the fact that the chief of the Titans is Chronos, also a Greek word for time. Chronos is infamous for castrating his father, Uranus, with a scythe[3] (which seems a bit of overkill) and eating his own children.[4] Viewed through the lens of *chronos* then, time is not simply a constant reminder of our finitude. Since everything is under its rule, chronos kills and devours us, an idea that becomes more vivid as the ancient myth of Chronos evolves into the Grim Reaper with his scythe.

If this is the only account of time available, Blue Oyster Cult gives us bad advice in their song "Don't Fear the Reaper." Fortunately, another temporal reality exists and is designated by a different Greek word for time: *kairos*. As we will use the term here, kairos refers to an opportune moment or redemptive time.[5] So when Jesus begins his ministry, he says, "The time is fulfilled" (Mk 1:15). Paul reminds us that God's saving word was revealed "in due time" (Titus 1:3) and that "while we were still weak, at the right time Christ died for the ungodly" (Rom 5:6). Thus, while chronos inexorably nudges us toward death, God's kairos disrupts clock time in order to bring life. Christianity is often described

---

[3]Hesiod, *Theogony*, in *Homeric Hymns, Epic Cycle, Homerica*, trans. H. G. Evelyn-White, Loeb Classical Library, vol. 57 (London: William Heinemann, 1914), 3. This is, by the way, why many depictions of Father Time picture him with a scythe.

[4]"These [children] great Cronos swallowed as each came forth from the womb to his mother's knees with this intent, that no other of the proud sons of Heaven should hold the kingly office amongst the deathless gods." Hesiod, *Theogony*, 9.

[5]I have used *kairos* and *chronos* to distinguish between two different ways that time can be understood. I recognize that while the New Testament offers a similar distinction between these terms in some places, *kairos* and *chronos* are used interchangeably in other passages. See James Barr, *Biblical Words for Time* (London: SCM Press, 1962), 20-46.

as a historical religion, in which God enters time and is involved in events. However, God's sovereignty means that time imposes no obligations on God. Time is God's plaything, so when God enters history, he also messes with it and allows us to experience fragments of eternity.

TOO SOON?

Why can't Mennonites tell jokes? Timing.

A man was savagely mugged, pistol-whipped, and robbed by a merciless thief. The first person on the scene was a psychologist, who looked at the semiconscious and badly injured victim in a puddle of blood and said, "How can this be? Whoever did this really needs help!"

Timing is important in humor. The cadence of the delivery, the skillful pause before a punch line, and the flow between the laughter and the segue to the next joke are all necessary skills for the professional comedian. However, comedic timing is not just about delivery. An occupational hazard for those doing standup is knowing when it is safe to offer a humorous take on recent tragedy. If the pain is still fresh, the audience will often groan rather than laugh, which usually results in the comedian's response, "Too soon?"

The psychologist in the previous joke is certainly correct that anyone who commits a brutal crime against another human needs help, but his timing is way off. Likewise, in view of the pervasive evil of this age, many early Christian leaders said the present was an inappropriate time for laughter. It's too soon. Augustine said, "Let us therefore understand, and make a distinction between those two times of fearing and laughing. . . . For so long as we are in this world, not yet must we laugh, lest hereafter we mourn."[6] Basil the Great stated that laughter is

---

[6]Augustine, *Expositions on the Psalms*, Psalm 52:9, *New Advent*, www.newadvent.org/fathers/1801052.htm.

never appropriate in this life since "never is he [Jesus] found to have used laughter."[7]

I'm not going to disagree with two saints, Augustine and Basil, about the propriety of mourning the fallenness of this age. Still, the epistle to the Hebrews reminds us, "You [God] have put all things in subjection under his [Jesus'] feet. For in subjecting all things to him, He left nothing that is not subject to him. But now we do not yet see all things subjected to him" (Heb 2:8 NASB). In this paradoxical passage, the panoramic view provided by kairos tells us that the subjection of all things to Jesus is a done deal. Yet, in chronological time, "we do not yet see all things subject to him." Where does this leave the believer? Is now a time of laughter, or is it too soon?

This "already but not yet subjected" situation presents an incongruity, and laughter often arises from the clash of seemingly incompatible realities. However, not every incongruity is funny. If I would arrive home to find a rhino in my living room, it is incongruous but not funny at all. However, if somehow I escape this situation unscathed, it is likely that afterwards I will recall this situation with laughter. The difference, as noted in chapter four, is distance; temporal distance gives us a new perspective on matters. One definition of comedy is that it is simply the combination of tragedy and time. It's tragic if your camper comes unhitched from your vehicle and is totaled, but years later, you have enough temporal distance that you can laugh about it—as long as Grandma wasn't riding in the camper. With enough time, people usually are able to look back on adolescent traumas and get a chuckle over their youthful angst. In both cases, the pain was real, but time allows us to see things differently.

I went to the library to check out a book on time travel. They wouldn't let me have it because I didn't bring it back.

---

[7]Basil of Caesarea, *The Rule of St. Basil in Latin and English*, trans. Anna M. Silvas (Collegeville, MN: Liturgical Press, 2013), 97.

God's invasion of clock time with kairos time makes Christians time travelers. With the resurrection of Jesus, we have already seen the future, and in a real way, we live there. We can only laugh at certain things in hindsight, but eschatological hope is a way of having hindsight. Thus, in response to whether this age is one in which laughter comes too soon, I argue that Christians should fully embrace a paradox. The sinfulness and evil of the current age, and every chronological age, is so profound that any trauma induced by mangled campers, zits, or being dumped by your first love pales in comparison. Because our sin occurs in the presence of a holy God, our mourning should be broader and deeper than those who do not recognize our offense to God. At the same time, Christ's defeat of death and evil has already happened, so our elation ought to surpass that of all people. After all, even if we don't get a new camper, God does give us the Holy Spirit and eternal life. I'll take that deal.

ESCHATOLOGY: IT'S ABOUT EVERYTHING

The only reason for time is so that everything doesn't happen at once.

ALBERT EINSTEIN

Our understanding of the present is determined by whether the future is present in the present. The Bible seems to say that the future is now. How can it be otherwise if our eternal God, to whom all future is present, is part of our here and now? This means that eschatology doesn't just pop up in a few passages scattered throughout Scripture. Wherever we find God's involvement with our world, we catch a glimmer of future redemption and resurrection. So eschatology isn't just about our time and God's eternity. It's about the juxtaposition of earthly kingdoms and God's heavenly kingdom. The "last things" concern the intersection of temporal forms of power and God's perfect power. We worship God and gods imperfectly here but anticipate the perfect worship of God later. Because Jesus' resurrection ushers eternity into our time, in God's funny way, everything is happening at once, and eschatology is as much about predicting the present as it is about anticipating the future. Thus, a big eschatology is one in which we attempt to put present things into their rightful perspective.

DELUSIONAL LAUGHTER

> An Edible: Good to eat and wholesome to digest, as a worm to a toad, a toad to a snake, a snake to a pig, a pig to a man, and a man to a worm.
>
> **AMBROSE BIERCE, *THE DEVIL'S DICTIONARY***

Eschatological laughter is not about amusement or brightening our mood. It is an expression of faith that God has saved us. End-times laughter reveals a sense of gratitude for the divine grace that blots out sin and grants eternal life. Alas, eschatological laughter is often confused with a spiritually dangerous form of laughter, laughter that arises from delusion, the delusion that only chronos time exists. Delusional laughter cannot see beyond earthly kings and kingdoms to catch a vision of a heavenly kingdom with its king. Earthly wealth frequently obscures our ability to see heaven's treasures. Thus, Jesus pronounces woes upon those who are rich, comfortable, well-fed, and laughing now (Lk 6:24-25) because they lack eschatological perspective. In God's future, they will weep, while those who have glimpsed God's long-term plan will be the beneficiaries of God's reversal and will laugh even though they weep now (Lk 6:21).

As is the case with all the goods God invests in his creation, those who possess political power straddle a dangerous fault line. These powers, if wielded benevolently, accomplish much good. However, they are also an intoxicant, and Scripture is filled with warnings to those who laugh drunkenly, convinced that their powers are their salvation. Acts 12 offers one example. King Herod has executed James, the brother of John, and then has Peter arrested. It looks like tyranny will win. However, before Peter can be executed, Peter is freed from his shackles and the prison by an angel of the Lord.[8] A higher king trumps Herod's play. A short time later, Herod went to Tyre and Sidon and wowed the audience with a speech that made them proclaim, "The voice of a god, and not of a mortal!" (Acts 12:22). Immediately thereafter, he was struck down and "was eaten by worms and died" (v. 23), a sequence that sounds particularly horrific. In a similar way, Israel is instructed to taunt the King of Babylon at his death.

> "You too have become as weak as we!
> You have become like us!"
> Your pomp is brought down to Sheol,
> and the sound of your harps;
> maggots are the bed beneath you,
> and worms are your covering. (Is 14:10-11)

The message to the powerful and pretentious is this: Chronos still devours those who acknowledge only earthly kingdoms. He just uses worms to do the job these days.

A Sunday school teacher, recapping her lesson, said, "The kings and queens of biblical times were very powerful, but we also learned that something is even more powerful. Can you tell me what is stronger than kings and queens?"

The teacher's pet in the front row raised her hand and said, "Aces!"

---

[8]There is an often overlooked humorous element in this story. After Peter flees prison, he goes to the house of John Mark's mother, where believers are praying for his life. When he knocks, Rhoda, the servant, comes to see who is at the gate. Upon seeing Peter, she runs back to the house and informs them that Peter is alive, leaving him locked outside. "Meanwhile Peter continued knocking" (Acts 12:16).

Satire, sarcasm, and mockery are the forms of humor found frequently in Scripture. In fact, one of the few explicit biblical references to God's laughter is Psalm 2:4 (compare Ps 37:13; 59:8), which states, "He who sits in the heavens laughs." The context is one in which earthly rulers conspire to wipe out the memory of God and his anointed one. In this case, God's mocking laughter is directed at the ludicrous overreach of those who think they have such power at hand. Author Joseph Grassi summarizes it as such: "When people plan, trusting only in human power, God laughs; when God plans, working through human weakness, people laugh."[9]

While God is the ace that tops any earthly king or queen, some of the most humorous events of Scripture occur when God uses his holy jokers—the prophets—to echo his scorn of those who suppose themselves to be mighty. In one of most sarcastic moments in Scripture, Ezekiel sings a funeral dirge to the King of Tyre—while the king is still alive (Ezek 28:12-19). He reminds the king that he had all that anyone could ever hope for at the beginning of his reign. This power could have been a force for good, but he squandered it all through his arrogance. This is a gutsy move on Ezekiel's part. Singing a dirge directly to the king's face is the equivalent of saying, "You are as good as dead." The prophet is smart enough to know that if you get into a staring contest with a corpse, you will lose. But Ezekiel also knows a deeper truth; even when it wins a staring contest, a corpse is still a corpse.

Some of the humor aimed at those who have earthly power is pretty, uh, earthy. While King Saul is pursuing David, he stops at a cave to "relieve himself" (1 Sam 24:3), and it just happens to be the cave where David and his men are hiding. Talk about getting caught with your pants down. My favorite, however, is when Ehud does in the morbidly obese Moabite king, Eglon, who had held Israel captive for eighteen

---

[9]Joseph A. Grassi, *God Makes Me Laugh: A New Approach to Luke* (Wilmington, DE: Michael Glazier, 1986), 14.

years (Judg 3:12-30). Since only his left thigh would have been checked for weapons by the king's guards, the left-handed Ehud was able to sneak in an eighteen-inch sword by concealing it on his right thigh. Once alone, Ehud drove his weapon so deep into Eglon's gut that the folds of his ample adipose tissue closed in and rendered it irretrievable. It gets worse. The sword thrust was so surprising that Eglon's "dirt" (don't make me translate that) came out. To top it all off, the king's servants did not check on him because the door to his "roof chamber" was locked and the overwhelming odor of his "dirt" caused them to suspect he was on that other, less royal, throne (Judg 3:22-24). By the time the servants realized that Eglon's problem might be a tad more severe than diarrhea and went to check on him, Ehud was long gone.

Church folk are often skittish about scatological humor, but perhaps we miss something critical when we err on the side of propriety. We need to be reminded that kings are as full of "dirt" as anyone else is, and it all pretty much smells the same. It may be crude, but it's true, and the spiritual consequences of forgetting this truth can be devastating. The power and lifespan of every person, emperor or slave, are limited and subject to God's judgment.

It isn't simply the pretensions of earthly rulers that are subjected to coarse mockery in Scripture. Idols and their fan clubs get the same treatment. For example, Jehu destroys the temple of Baal and turns it into a latrine for the city (2 Kings 10:27). However, my vote for most memorable use of indelicate prophetic mockery goes to 1 Kings 18:27. In the contest between Elijah and the 450 priests of Baal, Elijah razzes his rivals after they have, for several hours, strenuously pleaded for Baal to act, but to no avail. "Cry aloud! Surely he is a god; either he is meditating, or he has wandered away, or he is on a journey, or perhaps he is asleep and must be awakened." Spelling out the fact that a phrase usually translated as "he is on a journey" is a simply a polite circumlocution for "taking a dump" may be too blunt for a congregational reading. However, it may also be that we remain so enslaved to the Baals of our day because we have failed to rise to the level of full-throated mockery of false gods in whatever forms they invade our life. A crudely humorous assessment that refuses to pull punches may be exactly what we need to recognize the impotence of any god but God. If nothing else, it's obvious that God is serious about idolatry, as in second-of-the-Ten-Commandments serious, so this passage should put to rest the notion that one cannot be humorous, scatological, and serious at the same time.

While most scriptural criticisms of idolatry avoid bathroom humor, razor-sharp sarcasm remains a consistent feature. For example, Isaiah says of the foolish carpenter who plants a cedar, cares for it, and then cuts it down after it has matured:

> Half of it he burns in the fire; over this half he roasts meat, eats it and is satisfied. He also warms himself and says, "Ah, I am warm, I can feel the fire!" The rest of it he makes into a god, his idol, bows down to it and worships it; he prays to it and says, "Save me, for you are my god!" (Is 44:16-17)

Sarcastic humor peels the gold leaf off the idol and reveals it as nothing more than a common construction material, capable of providing a few BTUs to warm you and your pot roast on a cold morning but wholly unable to bring salvation.

THE NAME OF THE ROSE

 On the surface, she sounds really deep, but deep down, she's just shallow.

The plot of *The Name of the Rose*, one of the best-selling novels of all time, revolves around a long-lost treatise on comedy and laughter by Aristotle. The manuscript of this treatise has been discovered in the library of a Benedictine abbey in Italy. Jorge de Burgos, one of the older monks, wants to destroy it, believing that the esteemed philosopher's endorsement of laughter will make it respectable. Those who live in fear remain under the control of church officials, but laughter challenges fear and thus would undermine those Jorge considers the rightful authorities. William of Baskerville is a Franciscan who considers laughter to be godly and healthy, and he is resolved to stop Jorge.[10] In the end, the monastery is torched and Aristotle's treatise on laughter is lost forever. Nevertheless, William resolves to "make truth laugh,"[11] particularly at those who exert power over the powerless.

Both Jorge and William recognize the same truth. Satirical laughter is a potent weapon for undermining authority—political, ecclesiastical, social, or otherwise. This is why sarcasm, satire, and mockery so frequently appear in Scripture. God's people often exist on the fringes of society, and biting humor is one of the few tools available to oppressed people to counter the powers of oppressors. Stated in a slightly different way, this sort of weaponized humor always implies an eschatological power: judgment. Satire is highly moralistic; it judges that a moral or spiritual standard has been violated and deems this standard superior to those who wield power. Thus, it challenges convention and questions the way things are. If it amuses or entertains, that is simply a vehicle for the deeper aim of conviction, persuasion, and change.

The church has often been leery of humor, particularly genres such as mockery and satire since these intend to draw blood. Used rightly, however, laughing at the powers of darkness is a form of holy resistance. If nothing else, we need satire and sarcasm to remind ourselves of the humorous paradox that runs throughout the Bible: even though Egypt, Persia, Babylon, and Rome appear on the surface to be formidable forces, deep down their powers are shallow. Thus, laughing at taboos

---

[10]In an argument about the propriety of laughter, Jorge says, "Laughter shakes the body, distorts the features of the face, makes man similar to the monkey." William responds: "Monkeys do not laugh; laughter is proper to man, it is a sign of his rationality." Umberto Eco, *The Name of the Rose*, trans. William Weaver (New York: Harcourt Brace Jovanovich, 1983), 131.

[11]*Name of the Rose*, 491.

may be an effective way of recognizing that they never should have been taboo in the first place. However, we should also be reminded to aim satire's judgment at what is so often our favorite false god—ourselves. Until we can engage in a holy mockery of ourselves, scoffing at industrial-sized forms of idolatry is simply distraction and self-justification. If you need some help with this, God gives Job a primer (see Job 38-41) on how to proceed with satirizing one's self.

> A woman walked into an electrical-repair shop and said, "Can you help me? I think I'm a moth."
>
> The electrician said, "Why did you come here instead of going to a therapist?"
>
> The lady said, "That's where I was headed, but your shop had a light on."

Determining who is sane and who is delusional is not always a simple matter, and Revelation 5 offers an example of this difficulty. John has been exiled to Patmos by Rome (Rev 1:9), and the empire had turned its power against the church in a bloody persecution. When confronted by the massive military and economic dominance of the most powerful kingdom the world had ever seen, Christianity seemed doomed to extinction. But John reminds the believers that they have an advocate on their side.

The setting is the perpetual worship that goes on in God's presence, one that we join every time we meet here on earth for worship (Rev 4:1-11). No one can be found who is worthy to open the scroll and its seven seals that will release God's redemptive action. The seer of Revelation weeps in despair (Rev 5:4), but he is told that the Lion is worthy. Here's the crazy part: the Lion turns out to be a Lamb, and a battered and bloody one at that (Rev 5:6). As a symbol of power and honor, we would at least like to see a fearsome carnivore. Instead, we get a docile and bloodied ruminant. It's an unexpected punch line.

Rome versus a lamb. Whose claim to authority is logical and who is crazy? It seems to make more sense to buy into Rome's definition of power. Its military strength, organizational structure, and wealth created a realm that stretched onto three continents and had such longevity that it was referred to as the *imperium sine fine*, the empire without end. The small, ragtag band of Christians drawn mostly from the slave and lower classes was told to take hope from a bloody lamb who advocated love and sacrifice as forms of power. A main rule of eschatology is that time will tell us who's right, but we don't have to wait until the very end to get some clues. The *imperium sine fine* met its *fine*, although it took about four centuries after John wrote Revelation for Rome to completely sputter away. In contrast, the church, although often beleaguered and stumbling, continues preaching its message of love and sacrifice.

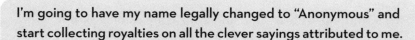

I'm going to have my name legally changed to "Anonymous" and start collecting royalties on all the clever sayings attributed to me.

Viracocha, Zhu Yijun, Unas, Asoka, Alexander Nevsky, Geta. Recognize any of those names? Unless you are a history dweeb, probably not. However, each was, at one time, an emperor, tsar, king, or Pharaoh. They each ruled millions, had fabulous wealth at their fingertips, and held their subjects' lives in their hands. They all had the forms of power wielded by Rome, but they are now footnotes in history books.

It is odd that we do not know the name of the Pharaoh confronted by Moses, even though he was a top-tier power broker of his age. However, we do know the names of the two common midwives, Puah and Shiphrah, who saved Moses and the other infant males born to Hebrew women (Ex 1:15-22). We know the name of Lazarus, a poor beggar, but the rich man who showed him no mercy remains anonymous (Lk 16:19-31). Granted, history is full of good and heroic Christians whose names have been lost to our memory. However, the names of the nobodies that have been preserved are a preview. We discover that God remembers all his people. So the divinely funny logic of God's redefinition of power ends in a reversal. The powerful and delusional who laughed in this life are thrown into the lake of fire and are forgotten (Rev 20:15), while those enrolled in God's book of life no longer remain anonymous but are known by name for eternity (Rev 3:5).

DARK HUMOR

A little later in the day I went to the library again to check out a book on how to commit suicide. They wouldn't let me have it because I wouldn't bring it back.

We tell jokes when we are desperate. One genre of desperate humor is gallows humor, which takes on taboo topics such as death, disease, and even suicide. Sometimes this humor seeks to momentarily divert our attention from impending disaster, like the criminals singing "Always Look on the Bright Side of Life" as they are being crucified in *Monty Python's Life of Brian*. Often, however, gallows humor recognizes the limited and finite nature of existence and takes a fatalistic and morbid turn, challenging people to come to grips with the inevitable. Thus, truly dark humor grows out of the awareness that chronos will devour us, but still puts up a defiant front by resolving to laugh in the face of time's tyranny. "Humor is just another defense against the universe," as Mel Brooks puts it. Defiant gallows humor is the only defense available if a silent universe neither knows nor cares about our existence or nonexistence. This type of humor may be resolute in its resistance, but it knows it cannot win.

I'm like a ripe stool, and the world's like a gigantic anus, and so we're about to let go of each other.

MARTIN LUTHER[12]

[12]Martin Luther, *Table Talk*, in *Luther's Works*, vol. 54, ed. and trans. Theodore G. Tappert (Philadelphia: Fortress Press, 1963), 448.

Martin Luther writes these words to his wife, Katie, as his death approached. They are admittedly vulgar, and I'll leave it up to you as to whether vulgarity has a rightful place in Christian humor, although, as we saw in the previous section, it makes an occasional appearance in Scripture's humor. However, since we know that the darkness of the principalities and powers is real, our humor in this life should acknowledge the darkness. Luther saw his impending death and acknowledged it as the enemy that it is (1 Cor 15:26). We tell jokes when we are desperate, and we are never more desperate than when confronted by death. But we also know that Luther believed that this wasn't the last joke he would ever tell.

I have always found it interesting that the literature and movies celebrated by critics are almost always gritty, raw, and dark. Any resolution to the grimness is viewed as Pollyanna and unrealistic. However, I find it inexcusable that some Christians stop the script at the bleakest moment. This is a failure of eschatological hope, and I am convinced that Christians are susceptible to this because we don't distinguish between wishes and hope. Wishful thinking is the desire that our salvation will come from some unforeseen source. While wishes cling to the miniscule chance that the cavalry will ride in to save us, Christian hope is the confidence that Calvary has already rescued us. Wishes require that we strain our eyes to see something in the future that we have never seen before, but hope waits to see in its fullness what we have already experienced in part.

Christian hope hangs on Easter. As Paul puts it, "If for this life only we have hoped in Christ, we are of all people most to be pitied" (1 Cor 15:19). Without Easter's new life, our wishes for rescue are so far-fetched that the most logical game plan is summarized in the dark proverb: "Let us eat and drink, for tomorrow we die" (1 Cor 15:32). But Paul's hope is that with death's defeat, even our bodies of dirt (Gen 2:7), which are buried in dirt, putrefy, and deteriorate into dirt (Gen 3:19), once again receive God's breath and live (1 Cor 15:35-58).

Eschatology is generally translated as the "study of the last things," but perhaps a more accurate translation is "the study of who gets the last laugh." In the ultimate humorous reversal, we join in the mockery of our mortal enemy: "Where, O death, is your victory? Where, O death, is your sting?" (1 Cor 15:55). Those are, by the way, rhetorical questions, but only to those who have resurrection hope. Not only do we participate in the last laugh, but as God's final act, he creates a space appropriate to laughter—the new heaven and the new earth. In fact, since "mourning and crying and pain will be no more" (Rev 21:4) in the new heaven and new earth, I take it that their opposites—joy, flourishing, and laughter—must necessarily replace them.

ESCHATOLOGY AS COSMIC COMEDY

> Sin and grace, absence and presence, tragedy and comedy, they divide the world between them and where they meet head on, the Gospel happens.[13]

So many treatments of the end times portray eschatology as tragedy. To be sure, tragic elements are scattered throughout apocalyptic literature. The sun and moon are darkened (Mk 13:24). False prophets and messiahs delude many (Mk 13:22). In addition, we read of famines and earthquakes (Mk 13:8), lawlessness (2 Thess 2:7), and hundred-pound hailstones (Rev 16:21), among other catastrophic events. To top it off, Revelation speaks of the death of one-third of earth's population (Rev 9:15), and lots and lots of blood—"as high as a horse's bridle, for a distance of about two hundred miles" (Rev 14:20). Even if you read all this metaphorically, it is a metaphor for something really awful. Though they ultimately are defeated, evil and death are powerful enough, we know, to expect that their final convulsions will bring tragedy.

However, often overlooked is evidence that we should also view eschatology through the lens of comedy. In the classical tragedies, the

---

[13]Frederick Buechner, *Telling the Truth: The Gospel as Comedy, Tragedy, and Fairy Tale* (New York: Harper & Row, 1977), 71.

heroes are bigger-than-life figures who embark on epic journeys and heroic tasks. In contrast, the stories of comedic heroes follow plot lines that are steeped in the mundane: unrequited love, a daughter's worthless suitor, or betrayal. The tragic hero is trapped by unbending moral standards and fate, and he dies in the final act. Comedic heroes, by contrast, are flawed individuals who, through offense and stupidity, inevitably trap themselves in sticky situations. However, the comedic entanglements are resolved in forgiveness, reconciliation, and a happy ending. Tragedy punishes, but comedy brings restoration, although the restoration process is often messy. In fact, you get the sense that the comedic playwright wants the comic lead, though imperfect and warty, to come out on top. For comedy, the door of grace swings open for undeserved redemption in a way that tragedy would interpret as injustice. So, should our experience of forgiveness look more like comedy or tragedy?

Another reason it seems proper to interpret Christian eschatology through the filter of comedy is that this genre often ends with a wedding. It is not just the contemporary romcom that concludes with a marriage between a flawed or decidedly average but lovable central character and a desirable mate (think *Hitch* or *Mall Cop*). That your everyday Joe wins the love of his life is a mainstay throughout comedy's history. For example, both of Aristophanes' comedies, *Peace* and *Birds*, end with weddings. However, the king of comedic marriages is none other than William Shakespeare. And some of his comedies conclude with multiples marriages, as in *A Midsummer Night's Dream, As You Like It, Much Ado about Nothing, Two Gentlemen of Verona, Love's Labor's Lost, Twelfth Night*, and *The Merry Wives of Windsor*. Marriage, as one of the highest expressions of human love, provides the comedic happy conclusion.

The funny thing is that Revelation also ends with a wedding. A church that is flawed and unremarkable becomes the bride of Jesus (Rev 19:7-9). Except here again we see a reversal. Instead of the groom being the lovable but ambiguous figure, in the marriage between Christ and his church, it's the bride who is iffy. The message is unmistakable: we have definitely married up. As believers, we are united with a groom we obviously do not deserve. And the groom is good with this and desires it. So in Christian eschatology, the big ending is the wedding (Rev 19:9). And, as everyone knows, weddings are times of feasts, "feasts are made for laughter" (Eccles 10:19), and wedding feasts were made for the chicken dance.

We are used to the either/or world that demands that what appears on the stage before us is either tragedy or comedy. God simply smiles and does things his own way. Although they seem to cancel each other out, both tragedy and comedy occur on the world's stage at the same time. But those who already experience God's redemptive power seeping back through this age's cracks know that the comedic word of forgiveness and reconciliation will be the final act. As Peter Berger puts it, "Redemption will finally be experienced as comic relief on a cosmic scale, and even now, in an as-yet-unredeemed world, redemption can be anticipated as a healing joke."[14]

A HUMORLESS HEAVEN? A BIT OF SPECULATIVE THEOLOGY

> It's always darkest just before the dawn, so if you want to steal your neighbor's newspaper, that's the best time to do it.

Much of the Bible's eschatological literature is shrouded in mystery, and I won't even pretend to know how properly to interpret the details. Still, I am confident that I know two main points about these writings. First, these apocalyptic materials, unsurprisingly, made their appearance during the bleakest of times: exile, captivity, and persecution. Their clear message is that, regardless of how dark and hopeless

---

[14]Peter L. Berger, *A Rumor of Angels: Modern Society and the Rediscovery of the Supernatural*, expanded ed. (New York: Anchor, 1990), 171.

circumstances seem, God's dawn is coming, so we need to stand fast (1 Thess 4:16-18). In other words, eschatological literature reminds us that God is in control of the future, and the future is a better indicator than the present of how we should understand the present. Second, although we may not understand how it can happen, heaven and earth will be reconciled. Revelation 11:15 tells us, and Handel helps us sing it in *The Messiah*:

> The kingdom of this world;
> Is become
> The kingdom of our Lord,
> And of His Christ,
> And of His Christ

It is the reconciliation of heaven and earth leading me to speculate that humor may not exist in heaven. Don't misunderstand me. I expect riotous laughter and lots of joy, almost unimaginable joy, to be prominent features of heavenly existence. I can hardly imagine a desirable eternity without them. But I'm not sure humor has a place in heaven, or perhaps to be safer, I don't see our beatific vision as including certain types of humor.

This might seem odd since I'm a big fan of the humorous in this life. However, if I'm right about why we might doubt that humor exists when we enter God's presence, the absence of humor is a good thing. If heavenly existence is one in which sin is no more, humor may also cease to exist. It's not that humor itself is sinful. However, it may be that humor is the *result* of sin and finitude.

Here's how it looks to me. As I have mentioned so many times throughout the book, much of our humor is rooted in incongruity. The coexistence of the supernatural and the natural *seems* to be incompatible to us. The incarnation, in which God takes on full and true humanity, *seems* logically incoherent. It *seems* irrational to believe that

God uses the world's losers to spread the gospel, that God would love us while we were yet sinners, that we could be citizens of heaven at the same time that we are subject to local zoning ordinances, swine flu, and questionable fashion choices, that an embodied animal could have spiritual capacities, that we have eternal life and still worry about getting to the airport on time to make our plane, and . . . well, you get the idea. Christians are asked to believe all sorts of things that *seem* to be just plain crazy, like the claim that heaven and earth will be reconciled. But if it is proper that the word *seems* should be italicized as a reminder that these things aren't really incompatible, contradictory, or just plain idiotic, the question is why they seem to be so incongruous.

I believe that I am both saved and sinner, that eternal life for all believers arises from the death of one, and all of the other paradoxes mentioned before. Humor confesses this, and in so doing, it also reveals that a part of me still struggles to grasp these truths. But I wonder if heaven is a place where the unity of everything that once seemed so contradictory is now so obvious that we laugh that we ever saw a tension between them. To be perfected in our humanity may imply that nothing that God does strikes us as odd or incongruent. Instead, what was once a divine surprise or stunning reversal is now completely expected: "Of course God does that." But who knows—God probably has a few more tricks up his metaphorical sleeve. I am confident that they will bring joy and laughter, but perhaps they won't be humorous in the way we now define it.

> Eschatology is a bit like a sermon. We know that the end will eventually come, but it seems like it should have happened sooner.

Meanwhile, we wait during Holy Saturday. As frustrating as it is not to know the when or how of God's consummation of all things, we know so much more than those who lived through the first Holy

Saturday. On that Saturday, the disciples were certain only of the bloody outcome of the previous day. However, because we have the advantage of hindsight, we also know that death was upended and Jesus' tomb was emptied out. Even though we still wait during our extended Holy Saturday, Easter Sunday's victory over evil and death gives us the foresight that tells us all we really need to know about eschatology. So while the disciples mourned the death of Jesus behind locked doors on that first Holy Saturday, we now live our extended Saturday with both Friday and Sunday in view. Nevertheless, even on Saturday we know that Sunday's humorous redefinition of Friday calls us to "a deep gladness of the soul that does not blink the reality of evil and tragedy, but interprets them in the light of a higher and deeper comedy."[15] Meanwhile, we wait during Holy Saturday, but with glad souls.

---

[15]Ralph C. Wood, *The Comedy of Redemption: Christian Faith and the Comic Vision in Four American Novelists* (Notre Dame, IN: University of Notre Dame Press, 1988), 3.

EPILOGUE

LAUGHING WITH GOD DURING EARTHQUAKES

 I like Jesus, but he loves me. It's awkward.

This book began with the observation that humor is one of the primary ways we communicate love. Used well, it signals openness toward the other and a willingness to build relationships. Humor is a way of saying that we have good intentions. I've argued throughout the book that, since Christian theology often uses the same tools that are essential to comedy, humor is one of the ways God communicates love to us. When we encounter Scripture's use of paradox, political satire, reversal, irony, and incongruity, we should hear it as a love language through which God invites us to laugh along with him, even when we are the targets of divine laughter.

When I started this project, I expected that a theological investigation would deepen my love and gratitude toward God. Making a conscious effort to reflect on God's faithfulness and forgiveness should do that. Greater love for God is, after all, the primary aim of good theology. Moreover, since humor is a conduit through which we experience love, I anticipated that examining the work of a gracious God through humor's filter would make God's love even more clearly visible. With gratitude, I can say that investigating the links between humor and theology has been spiritually enriching. What I didn't anticipate, however, was that this journey would confront me with an idea I had never considered. As I read theology through the lens of humor, I discovered that I don't just love God. I *like* God.

The idea of liking God initially struck me as so odd that I began to explore whether others had thought about this. You can find almost anything on the internet, but if you Google "Can we like God?" you get a lot of "Can we be like God?" or "Can we, like God, . . . ?" but you won't find much discussion of the original inquiry. As I have wrestled with this question, I've concluded that we should like God, even though it still feels a bit uncomfortable for me to say it. I think I've figured out a couple of reasons for this uneasiness.

First, liking God seems incompatible with the respect and awe that should be our proper response toward the transcendent one. It is certainly not my intention to downplay the vision of a God so holy that his people refused to speak the divine name for fear of displaying a lack of respect. There is a worship of God that demands that we fall on our face in holy fear and awe. As right and necessary as this reverent posture is, we also know a God who is called by the name of "Abba, Father" (Mk 14:36; Rom 8:15; Gal 4:6), a label that denotes intimacy and trust. Our understanding of God becomes unbalanced if we do not quake before the God of the burning bush, but is it any less unbalanced if we fail to see God as the smiling parent? So here is our final apparent incongruity: maybe the sovereign and exalted YHWH is also a likable daddy.

A second factor that makes us uncomfortable with the idea of liking God is that it may imply, as in the silly quip to begin this epilogue, that liking is a step down from loving. Certainly, no Christian wants to create the impression that they're demoting God from the "love" to the "like" category. Seen from a different angle, though, liking adds something to love. There are people that I love, but I don't want to be around them too long because, to be quite honest, I just don't like them that much. I've never stopped loving my wife, but situations have arisen when I couldn't truthfully say that I liked her at the moment. But when amends were made and I could both love and like her again, it was better. Liking augments loving. That seems obvious when you think about how difficult it is to love unlikable folks. It's not much of a challenge to love the people you like.

One thing that makes me believe it's proper to like God is that Jesus informed his disciples that they were no longer servants. Instead, "I have called you friends, because I have made known to you everything that I have heard from my Father" (Jn 15:15). I'm assuming that this promotion from servant to friend also applies to disciples of every age. We do, after all, sing "What a Friend We Have in Jesus." My friends are not my friends because I love them, although I do. Instead, they are friends because I like them and take pleasure in being with them. So if I'm friends with Jesus, and with God through Jesus, it makes sense that I should like God.

I love God for what he has done for us, but I also like God for the way God does it. When God makes the crown of his creation out of dirt, continually uses the least likely for his most important jobs, draws us near through bread and wine, and sneaks into the world as an infant, it is the sort of good-natured fun that makes me want to spend time with this God. I can't help but like a God who brings a mighty nation into being through an elderly, barren couple and preserves that people with an assist from a beauty-pageant winner. When God extends forgiveness and grace to those who don't deserve it, stands up for the powerless, and brings victory through sacrifice, I detect a winsomeness that enhances my enjoyment of the time I spend with God. I don't always understand God, but when I look at the way he does things through the filter of humor, I can't help but think of God as likable. I love this God, but I also like him so much that I want to be with him.

One final difference between loving and liking is worth consideration. Some of my friendships are what Aristotle called friendships of amusement.[1] These are relationships in which I enjoy being in a person's company simply because they are fun to be with. However, I may not

---

[1]Aristotle discusses friendship in book VIII of *Nicomachean Ethics*. In addition to the two types of friendships I mention here, Aristotle also speaks of friendships of utility, in which we form bonds with others because the relationship is of mutual benefit to both parties.

share the same values and goals of these friends. They make me smile, but I don't want to emulate them. My deeper friendships, however, are what Aristotle called friendships of virtue. These friends possess traits and dispositions that I find admirable, and I desire to spend time with them in the hope that I can absorb some of these virtues. These are friendships formed for the sake of becoming a better and more complete person. In addition to this, friendships of virtue are a two-for-one deal. They also, like the first form of friendship, provide amusement because as we grow in the virtues that allow us to flourish, these dispositions become pleasurable to us. Since the character qualities displayed by virtuous friends originate in God's goodness, I like God by liking these friends.

In sum, when I see God acting in ways that appeal to my sense of humor, I like this God. And it's not the quick click-of-the-mouse Facebook kind of like. It's a form of liking that allows me to enjoy spending time with God and creates a hunger to be more like God. As with my human friends, God doesn't intend to evoke laughter every time I'm with him. However, I want to be with God because he has at times spoken to me through his love language of humor, and he has made me laugh.

We had just returned from China with Zoe, the beautiful ten-month-old girl we had adopted. This was my first go-around at parenthood, and all the typical new-parent anxieties were augmented by the fact that we were all jet-lagged and wide awake at 2 a.m. Zoe was lying on our bed, and, not knowing what parents are supposed do in this situation, I started bouncing the mattress playfully. She started grinning. So I rocked it harder, and she started laughing. At full crescendo, I was on all fours, bouncing the bed and yelling "earthquake!" Her face was beet-red with laughter—the type of laughter I call "angel music"—and I knew that, regardless of what might happen in the future, we would be okay as long as we could laugh together.

The world for children is mysterious and frightening. So much is beyond their understanding and, in their powerlessness, they feel vulnerable and crave to be with someone they trust in moments of uncertainty. When vulnerability overwhelms them, they cling to you and cry. In other moments, something beautiful happens. A situation that could easily be interpreted as dangerous, such as a wildly undulating mattress and semi-maniacal vocalizations from a person completely unknown to you just days earlier, is defused by trust. Zoe's faith in my good intentions was the only difference between horror and laughter.

As God's children, we too often experience the world as frightening and horrible, and we understand enough to know that much is indeed dark and destructive. In these moments, we cling to God and shed our tears. This is appropriate. It is just as appropriate, though, to laugh with God. Our heartiest laughs are not a form of escape, amusement, or diversion. Instead, they are profound theological statements in which we confess our faith in a God who is faithful to us. In our laughter, we proclaim that the sovereign I AM will rout the principalities and powers because he is also the loving *Abba* who has the best of intentions for his children. In our paradoxical existence as saved sinners who straddle disease and eternal life in a world filled with earthquakes of all kinds, we can laugh because the I AM *Abba* wants to laugh with us. That is, after all, the purpose for which he has created us.

SCRIPTURE INDEX